HOW THE WORLD WORKS
PSYCHOLOGY

HOW THE WORLD WORKS
PSYCHOLOGY

*From spirits to psychotherapy: tracing
the mind through the ages*

Anne Rooney

ARCTURUS

Picture Credits

We have made every effort to contact the copyright holders of the images used in this book. In a few cases we have been unable to do so, but we will be very happy to credit them in future editions.

The Advertising Archives: 74

The Bridgeman Art Library: 12, 19 (Biblioteca Estense, Modena, Italy), 20 (British Library Board), 54, 101 (Peter Newark American Pictures), 144 (Fitzwilliam Museum, University of Cambridge, UK), 192b (Archives Charmet), 198 (Archives Charmet), 199t

Corbis: 10 (adoc-photos), 27b (Rick Friedman), 32 (Christie's Images), 35 (JACOPIN/BSIP), 40 (Bettmann), 47b (Bettmann), 64b (Bettmann), 65 (Bettmann), 73 (Bettmann), 80 (Bettmann), 81, 86 (Fine Art Photographic Library), 99 (Leemage), 102 (GraphicaArtis), 106t (Historical Picture Archive), 123 (Eric Raptosh Photography/Blend Images), 128 (ClassicStock), 132 (Graham Dean), 148 (Bettmann), 162 (Franklin McMahon), 166 (Hulton-Deutsch Collection), 175 (Hulton-Deutsch Collection), 180 (The Gallery Collection), 182 (Sunset Boulevard), 195 (The Gallery Collection), 197, 202 (Bettmann)

Fred the Oyster: 173

Getty: 14 (CM Dixon/Print Collector), 15 (CM Dixon/Print Collector), 59 (Fotosearch/Stringer), 118 (Thomas D. McAvoy/The LIFE Images Collection), 146 (Yvonne Hemsey/Getty Images), 155 (Nina Leen/The LIFE Picture Collection), 172 (Gjon Mili/The LIFE Picture Collection), 177 (NY Daily News Archive), 183 (United Artists)

iStock: 38, 51

The Kobal Collection: 90 (Warner Bros), 169 (TWO ARTS/CD), 178 (RAT PACK FILMPRODUKTION)

Mary Evans: 39 (INTERFOTO/Friedrich), 201 (Peter Higginbotham Collection)

Science and Society Picture Library: 49

Shutterstock: 21, 25, 27t, 30, 36, 46, 47t, 48t, 48b, 57t, 57b, 61, 62, 66, 76, 77, 78, 79, 84, 85, 89, 91l, 94, 95, 96, 97, 100, 104, 107, 112, 114, 115, 116, 117, 122, 130, 134, 145, 150, 151, 154, 159, 164, 165, 168, 179t, 194, 196, 203t

Topfoto: 18 (The Granger Collection), 108t, 143t (The Granger Collection)

Wellcome Library, London: 6r, 22, 24, 26r, 34, 37, 41, 42, 43, 44, 50, 52, 75, 91r, 92, 93, 121, 136, 137, 138, 139, 140t, 140b, 141, 142, 152, 184b, 185, 187t, 187b, 192t, 200

ARCTURUS

This edition published in 2017 by Arcturus Publishing Limited
26/27 Bickels Yard, 151–153 Bermondsey Street,
London SE1 3HA

ISBN: 978-1-78428-666-8
AD004015UK

Printed in Malaysia

Contents

THE STUDY OF MANKIND

'The proper study of mankind is man.'

Alexander Pope, *Essay on Man* (1732–34)

'Psychology' means 'the study of the soul'. Modern psychologists are more likely to talk of the 'mind', but in either case it is the nebulous, ineffable thing that animates the body, that is the agent of thought, feeling, creativity, doubt, inner struggle and myriad other activities. The modern working definition of psychology is 'the study of behaviour and mental processes'. The inclusion of behaviour is important, as behaviour undeniably exists, no matter what we might decide the mind is or is not.

The Reunion of the Soul and the Body *by William Blake (1808).*

The science of human nature

In the 18th century, the Scottish philosopher David Hume (1711–76) set out to devise a 'science of human nature' that would be as logical and empirical as the physical sciences set out by the astronomer Galileo Galilei (1564–1642) and the physicist Isaac Newton (1643–1727). He determined also that it would be an experimental science, though not in quite the same way that physics could be experimental, varying one condition or another and observing the results. The experimentation would lie in the observation of experiences and how they relate to each other and to behaviour. It took another hundred years for his dream to be realized. The study of psychology in the modern sense began in 1879 when the German physician and philosopher Wilhelm Wundt (1832–1920) set up the first psychology laboratory in Leipzig in Germany. Wundt was also the first person to describe himself as a 'psychologist'.

It would be wrong to assume that because

Wilhelm Wundt in 1898.

there were no self-labelled psychologists there was no psychology before 1879, though. Serious scholarly interest in the nature and working of the mind began with the ancient Greeks or even earlier, and the subject features also in the writings of ancient China. It might be fair to say that the earliest psychology text is by the Greek philosopher Aristotle (384–322BC), entitled *De Anima* ('On the Soul'). For more than two thousand years, psychology was a branch of philosophy.

The Story of Psychology will trace psychology through its origins in philosophy to its present-day merging with many other disciplines.

The subject matter of psychology

To say that psychology is the study of the mind and mental processes is to tell only half the story, however. The brain and the nervous system are clearly involved in mental activity. But more than that, psychology is concerned with behaviour and perception, with reflex actions and physical needs, and with how mental and physical states interact. It can also be concerned with evolution, and how mental adaptations help humans to survive and thrive. It is about what makes us individuals and what we have in common as human beings. It can involve studies with animals (comparative psychology). It can take place in a laboratory, out in the world, or inside an individual's head. In some ways, psychology involves all of human life. It is about the human condition, and what it is to be human.

Is psychology a science?

Hume set out to establish a new 'science' but it's hard to say how far psychology can be considered a 'proper' science. For one thing, there is no universal agreement on what constitutes science and how it should progress. For another, some aspects of psychology are more amenable to scientific

WELCOME TO THE BRAIN

The earliest appearance of a word for 'brain' is in the Edwin Smith papyrus, the earliest known medical text. Written in Egypt around 1500BC, but probably a copy of a much older text, the papyrus describes 48 cases of trauma and how to treat them. Most seem to be the result of falls or battle injuries. There are 27 cases relating to head injury, and many of these refer to the brain, the meninges (the membranes surrounding the brain) and cerebrospinal fluid. The convoluted surface of the brain is described as being 'like those corrugations which form in molten copper' (Case Six). Although it does not deal with psychology per se, the text recognizes the impact of brain and spinal injury on the rest of the body.

investigation than others.

The traditional model of science has been an endeavour that begins with empirical observation (something we have noticed about the world) and proceeds through inductive reasoning to explain it and propose rules (construct a theory) that will allow us to make predictions. The predictions are tested experimentally. If they turn out to be correct, the theory is reinforced, becoming stronger. If the predictions turn out not to be correct, the theory must be modified or discarded. At any point, a new observation might overturn the theory.

That traditional view has been challenged, though. The Austro–British philosopher Karl Popper (1902–94), argued

7

that instead of starting with observations, scientific enquiry should start with a problem that we want to solve, and that this guides empirical observation. Most importantly, he claimed that a theory must be 'falsifiable' – capable of being proved wrong. To this end, any scientific theory must be able to state in advance which results or observations would prove it to be false. Suppose we have a theory that all swans are white (as people once believed). This would be falsified the moment we found a swan of a different colour.

A 'paradigm shift': this Copernican solar system (c.1600) places the sun at the centre of the universe.

Another challenge to the traditional model comes from the American physicist and philosopher Thomas Kuhn (1922–96). He believed that science is driven by 'paradigms'. A paradigm is a general framework that is universally or widely accepted. Research takes place within the confines of the paradigm. Occasionally, the paradigm is found to be inadequate. Then revolutionary change occurs – a 'paradigm shift'. For example, for many centuries, astronomy progressed on the basis of the

geocentric model, which placed the Earth at the centre of the universe. Eventually, it became increasingly difficult to fit observations to this paradigm. Copernicus' revolutionary new model, placing the sun at the centre of the solar system, represented a paradigm shift.

Can psychology fit these models of science? To some extent it can. But there will always be a problem with objectivity and provability when we are dealing with the behaviour or thoughts of others (or even of ourselves). People can lie, or act in a way that is designed to distort experimental results; experimenters often have to rely on subjective judgments; results are rarely exactly reproducible; some types of experiment or observation are unethical and so cannot be carried out. Whatever it is, psychology is not a neat, wholly objective science, unlike chemistry, for example.

Plenty to do

Psychology is a nascent discipline. Although there is still plenty to discover in all the sciences, psychology is more acutely aware than most that it still has a long way to go. There is much that we don't understand about the working and nature of the mind, and psychologists are still developing and experimenting with new methods of inquiry. In the last few decades, psychology has joined forces with many other disciplines. That gives it more potential to progress, but makes drawing a line around what still counts as psychology very difficult.

In the first chapter of this book we will look at how the mind (or soul) has been considered by philosophers and psychologists over the centuries; and then in chapters 2 and 3 at how evidence for psychological ideas and theories has been gathered. Chapters 4 and 5 look at the history of ideas about how we construct knowledge and how we learn. Chapters 6 and 7 consider how psychologists have thought about what makes us individuals and what unites us. The final chapter looks at the history of abnormal psychology and how it has been treated.

TYPES OF PSYCHOLOGY

The history of psychology from 1879 until the late 20th century was dominated by a series of approaches. These were, roughly in order of emergence:

Voluntarism – the first form of experimental psychology, pioneered by Wilhelm Wundt in Germany in 1879.

Structuralism – the British psychologist Edward Titchener (1867–1927) led a structuralist approach, adapted from Wundt, that tried to break down mental processes into their smallest indivisible elements.

Functionalism – in the USA, William James (1842–1910 [see picture on the right]) began to look at the 'how?' and 'why?' of brain function.

Psychodynamic – pioneered by the Austrian neurologist Sigmund Freud (1856–1939) in Vienna in the 1890s, psychoanalysis was the first psychodynamic method of therapy; it attempted to trace neuroses to repressed experiences and alleviate them through 'talking therapy'.

Gestalt psychology – reacting against the methods that broke mental processes down, the Czech-born psychologist Max Wertheimer (1880–1943) tried to see mental events 'holistically' (in the context of the whole body).

Behaviourism – beginning with the work of John Broadus Watson (1878–1958) in 1913, behaviourism focused only on observable physical behaviours and did not concern itself with mental processes.

Humanistic psychology – a reaction against negative and partial approaches to the human mind, humanistic psychology, begun by the American psychologist Abraham Maslow (1908–70), sought to celebrate and improve the human condition.

Cognitive psychology – a return in the 1950s to concern with mental processes such as learning, knowing and processing information, which began with the work of George A. Miller (1920–2012) and Ulric Neisser (1928–2012).

Social psychology – an approach that examines how the individual behaves in relation to others and in social situations, pioneered in the 1960s and 70s by the likes of Stanley Milgram (1933–1984) and Philip Zimbardo (b.1933).

In the late 20th century, psychology fragmented into many fields and also combined with other disciplines including neurophysiology, evolutionary biology, computing, linguistics and anthropology.

CHAPTER 1

The ghost in the **MACHINE:**
what and where is the mind?

'*For it is the same thing to think and to be.*'

Parmenides,
(born c.515/540–450BC)

For millennia, people have pondered the question: where and what is the thing we each identify as 'I'? Am 'I' just a physical body? If so, what makes the difference between a living person and a corpse? What makes one person so very different in character from another? A common response is that it is the mind, or perhaps the soul, that makes us what we are. On the other hand, many people have said that all we are is our physical body – there is nothing special, nothing else, and it is only the basic biochemical processes that mark the difference between life and death or distinguish between individuals. It is a question as old as culture, and central to psychology.

Facing page: *Is it possible to put our finger on the mind, 'soul', or whatever it is that exists beyond our physical body?*

Mind and matter

The way we use language suggests that the mind, or other locus of 'I', is not the same as our physical body. Phrases such as 'I felt myself do…' and 'I can't bring myself to…' suggest a split between the mind and body. This is a 'dualist' position – one that supposes there are two types of substance involved in a person. One is the physical matter that makes up flesh and bones, and even the brain. The other is something else – some type of inspiring spirit, energy, consciousness, soul or something similar.

If the mind and the body are separate, how are they related and how do they interact? This fundamental question runs through many issues discussed in psychology and its therapeutic applications in psychiatry and psychotherapy, and even in other aspects of medicine.

Some philosophers take the 'monist' view – that things can be explained in terms of a single reality or substance. There are two common 'monist' positions. One is 'materialistic' – that there is only the physics and chemistry of our bodies, and everything we consider to be a mental event is in fact produced by physical factors. There is no airy-fairy 'something else' that distinguishes the thinking human from an inanimate rock, toothbrush or computer. The

radical behaviourist psychologists such as the American Burrhus Frederick ('B.F.') Skinner (1904–90) held that the mind does not exist: we are only our bodies, and all we do can be described in terms of behaviour.

The opposite 'monist' position states that everything is a mental event and the physical counts for nothing at all (it might

---

DENYING THE GHOST

The phrase the 'ghost in the machine' was coined by the British philosopher Gilbert Ryle (1900–76). He used it disparagingly of the idea of a mind or soul (the ghost) in a mechanistic body (the machine), while rejecting Descartes' dualistic view of the mind and body as different types of 'stuff' (see page 20–23). Ryle saw the distinction between mind and body as a 'category error' – a most fundamental mistake that then led to further errors because of the way the argument was being framed.

An Aboriginal soul journeying to the other world.

THE MIND TRICKING THE BODY

The placebo and nocebo effects are well known in medicine, and show clearly how the mind can have considerable influence over the body. The placebo effect is healing apparently produced by a placebo – a treatment with no genuine physiological effect, such as a sugar pill, but which the patient believes to be efficacious. The nocebo effect is the opposite – an ill effect produced by something harmless. A particularly striking instance of the nocebo effect was reported in 2007: a young man took an overdose of a medicine he was receiving in a clinical trial, believing it to be an antidepressant. He suffered serious physical effects, until told that he had actually been part of the control group and was receiving – and had overdosed on – a harmless placebo. At that point, his symptoms rapidly disappeared. The nocebo effect is also behind the phenomenon of people falling ill and even dying when they know they have been the subject of a curse, and of the efficacy of the Australian Aboriginal execution method of 'pointing the bone'.

not even exist). This is the idealist position. A psychologist who takes this position explains everything in terms of consciousness and mental acts. The 18th-century Anglo–Irish philosopher Bishop George Berkeley (1685–1753) was a monist of this type: he claimed that the external world does not exist except insofar as it is being perceived by human consciousness.

In ancient Greece, before the time of Socrates (see following page), the soul was seen as that which distinguished a living person from a corpse. It was the 'spirit of life', but that was its only role. It was not held responsible for behaviour, thought, feelings, intellect or any of the other attributes of mind. Initially only humans were spoken of as having a soul. The soul did not go anywhere after death or have any supernatural connotations; it was simply the state of a living person to be 'ensouled'

and of a dead person to be lacking a soul. Slowly, the meaning of 'soul' changed so that it could apply to any living thing. In the 5th century BC, it came to be associated with virtues such as courage, and with some actions of the mind – principally higher motives such as a love of learning. The Greek philosopher Socrates (c.470–399BC) held the body to be responsible for desires, fears, beliefs and pleasures (as presented in the work of his pupil Plato). One role of the soul was to keep the body in check, policing its baser instincts. The soul was in this sense much the same as the reasoning faculty.

Three in one

Plato (c.425–c.348BC) proposed a three-part soul. The 'appetitive' soul is concerned with satisfying physical appetites – the body's desire for food, drink, sex, sensation. The 'courageous' soul is concerned with the emotions, including love, hate, courage, cowardice, fear, rage and so on. The 'rational' soul seeks knowledge. The rational soul spends a good deal of its time trying to keep the other two in check, with varying degrees of success. In *Phaedo*, Plato uses the allegory of the charioteer to explain the relationship between the three aspects of the soul. The rational soul is the charioteer, trying to steer a chariot – body and soul – pulled by two horses, one white and one black. The black horse is the appetitive soul, and the white horse is the courageous soul. The black horse is trying to pull the chariot towards fine dinners and whore-houses while the white horse is pulling it towards acts of valour and benevolence, such as enlisting in the army. The rational soul tries to control the two as it negotiates the best course.

Aristotle proposed a different trio of

> *'What is it that, when present in a body, makes it living? — A soul.'*
> Plato's *Phaedo* ('On the Soul')

souls. He believed that each animate thing, from plant to human being, has a soul that is suited to its function and has capabilities and duties appropriate to the organism. This might include abilities such as growth (in a plant) but also locomotion (in an animal) and abstract reasoning (in a human). In this, Aristotle approached modern concepts regarding the function of the brain and mind. The brain does regulate voluntary and involuntary activities such as breathing and moving, and is also the site of non-physical activities such as contemplation, desire, reasoning and thought. Aristotle, unlike

HEART AND SOUL

It might seem obvious to us that the brain is the part of the body that does the thinking, feeling, dreaming, believing and other mental activity. But until recently there was nothing to be seen in the brain that showed it to be doing those things, so earlier generations did not necessarily locate thought in the brain. The ancient Egyptians put the centre of emotions, reason and thought in the heart. Indeed, they discarded the brain when they mummified their dead, even though they carefully preserved all the other organs in Coptic jars for burial with the mummy.

The Greek philosopher Plato suggested that the brain was the site of thought, but his pupil Aristotle (384–322BC) rejected this, plumping for the heart once again.

Plato's allegory of the charioteer steering a black and a white horse explains the three-part soul.

Plato, did not believe the soul could survive the body or have any existence independent of it. In this, too, the Aristotelian soul is closer to the modern mind rather than a semi-mystical spirit.

In two minds

In Epicurean tradition, which is based on the teachings of the ancient Greek philosopher Epicurus (341–270BC), the soul has two parts: one rational, and one non-rational. The rational part, called *animus* (mind), produces emotions and impulses, applies concepts, forms beliefs, assesses evidence, interprets sensory perceptions, and so on. The non-rational part is responsible for receiving sense-impressions (sights, sounds, smells and so on), which it does accurately. Any errors arise later, when the rational part of the soul is interpreting them. The non-rational part also transmits impulses that originate in the rational part, and carries

out non-reasoning tasks. We don't regard our minds as being responsible for seeing or for keeping us breathing. These are rather pedestrian, practical tasks carried out by the brain, and are achieved also by animals that we would not usually assume to have a soul or conscious thought processes, such as hedgehogs and prawns (though we might be wrong about the hedgehogs and prawns).

The Stoics (see panel on page 16), members of a school of philosophy in ancient Athens, took the crucial step towards suggesting something like the prevailing modern view of the mind. They considered there to be three types of *pneuma*, or inspiring spirit. (The literal meaning of *pneuma* is 'breath'.) The most basic is present even in rocks. It holds solid matter together – a function scientists today would ascribe to the laws of physics and the behaviour of atoms and molecules. The next provides for the vital functions of plant life (growth, respiration and so on). Finally, soul provides the mental and psychological functions of animals and humans. It varies in its capabilities according to the animal, so in a human it covers reason, belief, intellect and desire as well as the basic mental processes such as sensory perception.

The Stoic conception of the soul is not an animating spirit, the breath of life, or the difference between being alive or dead. It is a conglomeration of mental processes that provide awareness, understanding, thought, consciousness and meaningful interaction with the world.

Soul-grabbers

With the rise of monotheistic religions, the soul was hijacked in the service of God. Now the soul became a shard of divinity resident in each body, reflecting or struggling towards a godhead.

The Neoplatonists, such as the Jewish philosopher Philo of Alexandria (20/25BC–AD50) and the Roman thinker Plotinus (204–270), adopted the more mystical aspects of Plato's thinking and adapted it to religion. Philo melded Plato's division between sensory and rational aspects of the human with Hebrew religious teaching. He took as his starting point the Jewish model of the physical body imbued with a soul that is a fragment of the divine being. Unlike Plato, though, he did not believe that introspection and reason would lead to knowledge – that could come only from God, by divine inspiration. To prepare the soul for the gift of knowledge, Philo considered it necessary to meditate and to distance oneself from base appetites, so we should eschew bodily impulses. Philo believed that inspiration could also strike in dreams and trances, as these distance the Soul from the physical world. Plotinus saw the Soul as reflecting the Spirit, itself an image of 'the One'. This gives a three-part hierarchy, with the One at the top, imperfectly imaged in the Spirit, and the Spirit imperfectly imaged in the Soul. He taught that, in entering a body, the Spirit merged with something inferior.

The Platonic and Neoplatonic model of the soul struggling to master the bodily impulses was immediately accessible to Christian theology. It required only minor reworking to have the noble soul striving

---

THE STOICS

Stoicism was a school of philosophy begun by the Greek philosopher Zeno of Citium (334–262BC) in Athens in the early 3rd century BC. The Stoics held that destructive emotions such as hatred and envy come about through errors of judgment, and that only a wise man can be truly happy. Later Stoics included the Roman philosopher Seneca the Younger (4BC–AD65) and the Greek sage Epictetus (c.AD55–135).

towards godliness while the base body tries to drag it down to frolic in wayward pleasures. This tweaking was accomplished by the early Christian philosopher Augustine of Hippo (345–430). Eight hundred years later, the Italian priest Thomas Aquinas (1225–74) did the same tweaking and accommodation for Aristotle. In the main, though, the period following the fall of the Roman Empire was a fruitless one for the development of psychological thought in Europe. The soul/mind was in thrall to God and any interpretation of its workings was therefore theological. Instead, it was the Arab world that kept the flame of learning alight.

In the footsteps of the prophet

After the death of Mohamet in 632, Islam spread rapidly throughout the Arab and Persian world. Middle Eastern thinkers read the works of the ancient Greeks, particularly Aristotle, and wrote translations and commentaries on them. It was through Arab and Byzantine culture that Aristotle's writings resurfaced in Europe in the Middle Ages. For a period of around four hundred years, Middle Eastern culture made great strides in all branches of science – until Islam took a more intellectually conservative, curiosity-stifling turn in the 12th century.

One of the most important Islamic scholars was the Persian Ibn Sina (980–1037), who was known as Avicenna in the West. His work was firmly rooted in Aristotle.

In psychology, Ibn Sina is most famous for his 'floating man' thought experiment. Imagine that you have suddenly been created, from nothing, suspended in mid-air and without any sensory input from the environment or a body. Because it is possible to conceive of this existence, and to be thinking and conscious in this state, and not doubt one's existence, it is, he claims,

Philo of Alexandria reading to his students.

clear that the mind is a real thing separate from the body:

'Therefore the nafs [self, soul], whose existence the person has affirmed, is [his/her] characteristic identity that is not identical to the body nor the limbs... [Therefore] the affirmation of the existence of its-self (soul, al-nafs) is distinct from the body and something that is quite non-body.'

For his purposes, Ibn Sina required the soul to have sufficient connection with the

17

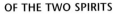

OF THE TWO SPIRITS

'God created man to rule the world, and appointed for him two spirits after whose direction he was to walk until the final Inquisition. They are the spirits of truth and perversity.

The origin of truth lies in the Fountain of Light, and that of perversity in the Wellspring of Darkness. All who practise righteousness are under the domination of the Prince of Lights, and walk in ways of light; whereas all who practise perversity are under the domination of the Angel of Darkness, however, even those who practise righteousness are made liable to error. All their sin and their iniquities, all their guilt and their deeds of transgression are the result of his domination…

It is to these things that all men are born, and it is to these that all the host of them are heirs throughout their generations. It is in these ways that men needs must walk and it is in these two divisions, according as a man inherits something of each, that all human acts are divided throughout all the ages of eternity.'

From the *Manual of Discipline*, the Dead Sea Scrolls.

body to be individual (not just a fragment of a universal soul), but sufficiently separate from it to survive bodily death. He followed the Greek physician and philosopher Galen of Pergamon (AD130–200) in believing that parts of the soul were localized in different parts of the body:

'In general, there are four types of proper spirit: One is brutal spirit, residing in the heart and it is the origin of all spirits. Another – as physicians refer to it – is sensual spirit, residing in the brain. The third – as physicians refer to it – is natural spirit, residing in the liver.

The fourth is generative [or procreative] spirit, residing in the gonads. These four spirits go between the soul of absolute purity and the body of absolute impurity.'

Ibn Sina, *Canon of Medicine* (1025)

The internal drama of good and evil

While the Arab world was developing Aristotle's ideas, his theories were lost to most of Europe until the 12th century. Even after they became available to Europeans again, it made little difference to the average person. In daily reality, the struggle going on inside each individual's mind and soul between the impulses to behave well or to follow the body's natural base urges remained essentially religious. On the one hand, the soul would strive towards God; on the other, the body was all in favour of having a good, self-indulgent time. The struggle within the mind to do what we know is right rather than what the body instinctively wants us to do is the one Aristotle addressed more than 1,500 years previously, but now cloaked in religious language.

Freeing the spirit

With the flowering of intellectual thought that came with the Renaissance in the 14th century, Europe finally set out again on the path of intellectual endeavour. Although people were still not free to think whatever they liked – there were plenty of heretics being burned – there was certainly more freedom for exploration and expression, as long as it was couched in ways that the Church did not regard as being too provocative.

As science was able to progress once more, it became more objective. Physical laws had been discovered that explained the path of an arrow or a cannonball and even the motion of the planets (around the sun, now, not around the Earth). The prevailing view was now that mathematical and scientific laws lay behind all natural phenomena and could be discovered through observation and reason. The notion that the world – indeed, the universe – was explicable was revolutionary. And if the movement of the planets, or the path of a cannonball were susceptible to investigation and explanation, why not ourselves?

IBN SINA (AVICENNA) (980–1037)
A child prodigy, Ibn Sina had memorized the entire Koran by the age of ten and was a physician at the age of 20. His expertise extended to many disciplines and he wrote nearly 450 books, of which around 240 survive. Forty of his works are on medicine, including aspects of mental health and the nature of the mind. His 14-volume *Canon of Medicine* was used in some European universities until 1650 – that's the equivalent of a modern university using a text book written around the time of the Black Death.

A page from Ibn Sina's Canon of Medicine.

One or two?

The French mathematician and philosopher René Descartes (1596–1650) was greatly influenced by the mechanistic approach to science and the world that was characteristic of the Enlightenment. Descartes himself had developed Cartesian geometry, a way of demonstrating the mathematical relationships between objects in three-dimensional space. In 1628, the English physician William Harvey (1578–1657) had explained the movement of blood through the body – implying that even the body was a type of machine. Descartes seized on this image. But what then was the soul, or the mind?

Descartes concluded that although the body is a material object, controlled by mechanistic laws, the spirit is immaterial. He assigned as much mental activity as possible to the body. So perception, memory, imagination and common sense were all to be explained in terms of the sensory organs and nerves. What was left – the uniquely human – was self-consciousness and language, and these were the functions of the spirit.

Allegorical medieval poems and plays depict the internal life through the personifications of sins, virtues and abstract notions such as The World or Death. The individual then has no responsibility for his or her internal state. The urge to sin is portrayed as an external assault on the soul, which is disempowered, becoming simply a battleground, trophy or hostage.

'It is one and the same man who is conscious both that he understands and that he senses. But one cannot sense without a body, and therefore the body must be some part of man.'

Thomas Aquinas, *Summa Theologiae* (1265–1274)

I doubt, therefore I am

Descartes sought to base his philosophical enquiries in some certainty he could trust. He discovered that the only thing he could be certain of was his own existence, leading to his famous dictum *cogito ergo sum* ('I think, therefore I am'). He arrived at this concept by realizing that all he saw or experienced might be no more real than a dream, but the very fact that he was doubting its veracity, and thinking about the issue, proved his own existence. This recalls the 'floating man' thought experiment of Ibn Sina around six hundred years previously.

As later critics pointed out, Descartes hadn't really proved his own existence. He had proved that thinking was going on, but not that he was doing it or that he existed because he was doing it. But it's good enough for our purposes, as his argument established a distinction between the physical and spiritual/mental identities.

The notion that thinking could take place without any sensory input from the body suggested a degree of separation between mind (or soul) and body. Descartes developed a model of body/soul dualism that, much later, the British philosopher Gilbert Ryle (1900–76) labelled the 'ghost in the machine' (see page 12). Still, the spirit had to be somewhere. Descartes decided that it resides in the pineal gland deep within the brain. But if it was immaterial, how could it be anywhere? How could it have an effect on the material body? And

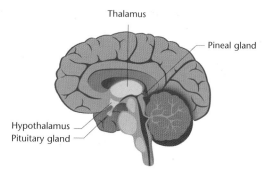

Thalamus

Pineal gland

Hypothalamus

Pituitary gland

THE ENLIGHTENMENT

The Enlightenment was a cultural movement that started in 17th-century Europe – particularly England and France. It promoted rational thought and empirical science, denounced superstitious thought and sought to challenge traditional ideas, rejecting them if they did not stand up to rigorous scrutiny. Key figures in the Enlightenment include the scientists Francis Bacon (1561–1626) and Isaac Newton (1643–1727), and the philosophers René Descartes, Baruch Spinoza and David Hume. We will meet the last three again shortly. The movement was closely tied to the Scientific Revolution, and marked the beginning of the modern period.

An Experiment on a Bird in an Air Pump (*1768*).

William Harvey's theory of circulation inspired Descartes' idea that the human body worked like a machine.

> 'The exploration of the globe having resulted in discoveries that have destroyed many of the data on which ancient philosophy reposed, a new conception of things will inevitably be called for.'
>
> Tommaso Campanella (1568–1639), Italian friar and philosopher

how could it be affected by the material body? It was clear to Descartes that there is an influence, in both directions, for an injury to the body (or bodily pleasure) has an effect on the mind, and moods of the mind are expressed through the body. This can happen in quite extreme ways: the physical manifestations of mental distress can look like bodily illness, such as trembling, nausea and pain in the stomach or head. Descartes was unusual for his time in considering there to be two-way traffic between body and soul. But he couldn't come up with an adequate answer to the question of how the immaterial soul and the material body could interact. Indeed, it is a question that remains unanswered.

Gottfried Leibniz (see panel on page 23) tackled the issue of how the mind/soul and body interact by saying that they didn't need to. Both follow independent deterministic paths, but these paths run in parallel. God set the two off on the same path and, like two clocks started together that keep perfect time, they will always be synchronized. Consequently, mental states and acts are always in accord with bodily sensations and actions.

The mechanism of the mind

Although Descartes saw the human body as mechanistic, he considered the soul or mind to be of a different substance. The English philosopher Thomas Hobbes (1588–1679) and the French priest and mathematician Pierre Gassendi (1592–1655) both went a step further in their adoption of the mechanistic model.

Gassendi saw no reason why Descartes should think the body obeyed physical rules but not the mind. Indeed, he saw no point in distinguishing between the mind and the brain at all and adopted a position of physical (or material) monism – there is only one type of 'stuff' and it is matter. He suspected that Descartes also thought this but was afraid to say so, as the Church would have taken a dim view of such a pronouncement.

Hobbes was also a thorough-going

materialist. He saw nothing in the universe besides corporeal matter, which he believed was governed by the mechanistic laws of nature, and considered metaphysics all bunkum. Hobbes contended that human actions, like those of animals, are entirely determined by natural laws and that these must apply to behaviour and thought as well as to obviously physical activities such as walking and breathing. He considered that thought progresses by rules, making ideas and knowledge from the stuff of sensory experience.

'Material monism' dispenses with the problem facing dualists such as Descartes of how an immaterial spirit can interact with a material body. If both mind and body are made of matter, there is no distinction between them, so there is no communication problem.

It's all one

The Dutch–Jewish philosopher Baruch Spinoza (1632–77) also denied that there is any special spiritual substance that makes up the mind. Spinoza denied quite a lot of things, including that God is a special being. For that, Spinoza was excluded from the Jewish faith and reviled by Christians. As we would expect from someone who wouldn't make an exception even for God, he didn't consider the human mind to be anything separate from the body, but for both body and mind/

MONADS

The German philosopher Gottfried Leibniz (1646–1716) had an original view of the world. He considered the universe to be made up of an infinite quantity of tiny points or life-units that he called 'monads'. These are present in all matter, including inert matter. Every monad is to some degree alive and conscious. As we move up a hierarchy of living matter from microbes to humans (and even to God) the quality of monads improves. Humans contain some high-quality human-soul monads, but also contain a mix of lower-order monads, so our thinking is not always lucid or accurate. Inert matter and microbes contain very low-grade monads and so are not capable of much thought. Even our top-notch monads have ideas only in the form of potentialities, which experience or sensory perception can cause to be actualized.

soul to be aspects of a single substance. His position, called 'neutral monism', regarded the whole of the universe as consisting of the same substance, but manifested in many different modes or modifications. Thus, the whole of nature, which was also equivalent to God, partook of consciousness. (This is a pantheistic and panpsychic position.) It was a neat solution to how mind and body can communicate: although they look different, they are actually two sides of the same coin.

Another monist option

Clearly, if mind/body dualism posits two types of stuff, material monism says there is only physical matter, and neutral monism says both are the same substance, then there is space for another type of monism that says there is only spiritual or mental 'stuff'. The position that states that thought or spirit is all and the material universe does not exist was espoused by philosophers such as Bishop George Berkeley. Immaterialism, or subjective idealism, argues that material reality is created by the observer and without

THE SEAT OF THE SOUL

Descartes had two reasons for supposing the soul resided in the pineal gland. At the time, it was considered one of the few parts of the brain that did not come in pairs (the pineal gland is now known to have two hemispheres). There is only one pineal gland and clearly, he thought, we can have only one soul. The pineal gland is also located near the ventricles of the brain, which contain cerebrospinal fluid. Descartes believed the body was controlled by the cerebrospinal fluid affecting the nerves, and sensations were carried from the nerves through the cerebrospinal fluid to the pineal gland. Sensations would make the pineal gland vibrate, producing emotions. The body's actions would then result from outgoing messages sent from the pineal gland. The pineal gland was the perfect seat of command for the soul to rule the body. Interestingly, in several mystical traditions the pineal gland is considered to be the 'third eye' that is important in spiritual experience.

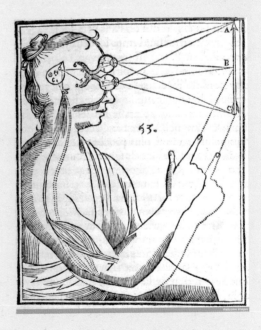

THE GHOST IN THE MACHINE: WHAT AND WHERE IS THE MIND?

an observer it has no meaning.

By the mid-18th century, all the main positions regarding the body and mind had been established: they are two different types of stuff (with communication problems); they are both the same physical stuff; they are both the same immaterial stuff; they are both different aspects of the same, global, stuff.

IF... THEN... The consequences of mechanistic models

Spinoza took a thoroughly deterministic view. In his model, everything happens according to the immutable laws that govern the universe, and this includes human thought and actions. Determinism means that there is no such thing as free will, even though humans believe they are acting freely. Instead, 'Men are conscious of their desire and unaware of the causes by which [those desires] are determined.' All mechanistic models tend towards determinism, for if the body and mind follow natural laws, all that happens is linked in an unbroken chain of inevitable consequences through time.

There is a serious consequence of this determinism, though. If all mental events and activity are determined and we have no freedom, how then can we hold a person responsible for their actions? Spinoza recognized this and saw that words such as 'blame' and 'praise' were entirely inappropriate, as everyone does what he or she has to do. The only kind of freedom is the freedom to see that we are constrained and understand why we act as we do. He postulated that moral concepts such

> '[The universe] is corporeal, that is to say, body... Also every part of body, is likewise body, and...consequently every part of the universe is body, and that which is not body, is no part of the universe; And because the universe is all, that which is no part of it, is nothing; and consequently nowhere.'
> Thomas Hobbes (1651)

as good and evil must have their basis in psychology. Many later psychologists, especially materialists and behaviourists, believed that we don't really have free will, but for different reasons. Any model that has our actions determined by past experiences or innate compulsions removes (or at best compromises) free will and responsibility.

The mechanistic mind as computer

The problem of responsibility and free will troubled the French mathematician Blaise Pascal (1623–62), too. He considered the

25

mind to be similar to a machine such as a computer (Pascal invented an early mechanical calculator), capable of incredibly complex calculations and operations, but ultimately reducible to logic and laws of information processing. One consequence of this view is that the human mind is no different from the mind of an animal, a conclusion Pascal was

Pascal's early mechanical calculator.

THE EMERGENCE OF NEUROLOGY

Thomas Willis (1621–75) was an English

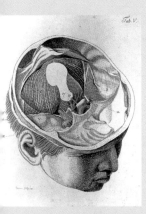

anatomist and a founding member of the Royal Society. His view of the mind/ body issue was firmly rooted in what he had learned from dissections and neurological studies, which led him to conclusions that are now common in neuropsychiatry and philosophy of mind. Now called 'supervenience', the model Willis described has every psychological aspect of the mind 'supervening' (depending) on an equivalent neurological aspect. So each mental state or act comes about (in modern terms) as a particular firing or connection of neurons in the brain, or a particular chemical response. The mind is not a separate entity, but a product of the neurological workings of the brain. This is remarkably similar to the view held today by the American philosopher John Searle (b.1932), that consciousness is an emergent property of neurons.

not happy with. To avoid this conclusion, he sought to make free will, instead of reason, the distinguishing feature of humanity. Unfortunately, his account of free will is not compatible with his ideas about the efficacy of God's grace, and he ends up with the position in which people are either saved or damned according to whether or not God gave them an irresistible urge to do the right thing. So they're not very free after all.

The model of the mind as a kind of computer, or information-processing machine, became very popular in the 1960s with the rise of computing. The ways in which a mind might be like a computer, or a computer like a mind, became a major concern of cognitive science. Going beyond psychology, cognitive science combines elements of computer science (particularly artificial intelligence, or AI), linguistics, psychology, neurology, anthropology, philosophy and any other discipline able to yield useful methods or insights. It is concerned with the nature of – and working cognitive processes in – human and animal minds and computers, covering

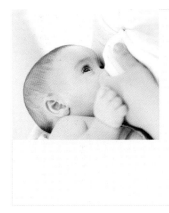

'The infant believes that it is by free will that it seeks the breast; the angry boy believes that by free will he wishes vengeance; the timid man thinks it is with free will he seeks flight; the drunkard believes that by a free command of his mind he speaks the things which when sober he wishes he had left unsaid…All believe that they speak by a free command of the mind, whilst, in truth, they have no power to restrain the impulse which they have to speak.'

Baruch Spinoza (1677)

how information is represented to the mind (perception), processed (understood and stored) and transformed (in, for example, recall and creative acts).

Not special at all

Modern philosophers of mind have had no such compunction about reducing the status of the human. The American philosopher Daniel Dennett (b.1942), who believes that all mental functions and activities are entirely the result of the physiology of the brain, even goes so far as to say that there is no difference between a human mind and the 'mind' of a supremely sophisticated computer. He claims that if we can make a computer that appears to be as intelligent as a human then it actually is as intelligent as a human – there is no meaningful distinction between human and machine intelligence, and we are very much a machine with no ghost.

Daniel Dennett in his office at Tufts University, where he is director of the Center for Cognitive Studies.

Losing your mind

The 18th-century Scottish philosopher David Hume (1711–76) agreed with Berkeley that we can never experience the physical world directly, we can only experience it as mediated through our senses. He did not deny the existence of the physical world, though – just that we have to take its existence on trust, since we have no way of testing reality. Hume went so far as to say that since everything we 'know' is based on our perceptions, we are nothing more than a bunch of perceptions. There is no such thing as the mind, just the sum total of our personal experiences and the links we have made with them:

'We may observe, that what we call a mind, is nothing but a heap or collection of different perceptions, united together by certain relations, and suppos'd, tho' falsely, to be endow'd with a perfect simplicity and identity.'

Not only is there only a bundle of perceptions where we are accustomed to seeing a mind, there is also, necessarily, no such thing as the 'self' separated from those perceptions. Hume would be extremely influential in the following centuries as perception came to be recognized as the interface between the world, the body and the mind, and indeed as the behaviourists also rejected the idea of a mind 'endow'd with…identity'.

Hume observed, 'I can never catch myself at any time without a perception' and that when perceptions are removed by sleep he was 'insensible of myself, and may truly be said not to exist'. On death, when his perceptions all end, he 'should be entirely annihilated'.

The tri-partite ghost revisited

A hundred years after Hume tried to dismantle the mind, leaving only his 'bundle of perceptions', the German neurologist Sigmund Freud (1856–1939), founder of psychoanalysis, brought it roaring back. His theory looks remarkably like Plato's charioteer reining in two wayward horses.

Id, ego and superego

Freud identified three parts of the psyche: the 'id', the 'ego' and the 'superego'. The 'id' is the most primitive, need-driven part and its energy, the 'libido', provides the impetus to satisfy needs immediately. The 'ego' is the voice of practical realism. It recognizes the drives of the id and tries to negotiate them in the real world, satisfying them as far as possible within the limitations of the physical world. The id acting alone would snatch a sandwich from a person in the street to satisfy hunger. The ego realizes that such behaviour is likely to get you into trouble – you might get punched or arrested – and sends you to buy your own sandwich. The superego adds morality to the mix. So instead of not stealing a sandwich because of the consequences, you learn not to do it because it is wrong. Without a superego, a human is much like any other animal (assuming animals don't have an idea of morality). The ego then has to negotiate three ways, between the drives of the id, the realities of the external world, and the value-led demands of the superego.

While the id and ego are innate, the superego is present in potential form in the baby, and is populated with values through the socialization of the growing child. As a child is rewarded for approved behaviour and punished for unapproved behaviour, the superego builds an internalized set of values. Successful socializing means that the individual will feel good if they do or even think about doing approved behaviours and will feel bad (guilty, ashamed, embarrassed) if they contemplate or carry out behaviours that are denigrated.

There is inevitably tension between the id, ego and superego as they have different goals. One of the coping mechanisms used by the ego is repression. If a desire of the id is going to cause problems if satisfied, or lead to anxiety if contemplated, it might be excluded from the conscious mind – repressed. Freud found repression of desires or memories at the root of all neuroses as the mind sidesteps the issue that can't be confronted or acknowledged.

Me, myself and I

While Freud was developing his ideas in Vienna, on the other side of the Atlantic, the pioneer of American psychology, William James (1842–1910), was setting out his theory of the self divided into two: 'Me' and 'I'. The 'Me' self was then subdivided into a further three parts: the material, social and spiritual 'Me'.

The material self comprised the things belonging to the self, or that the self belongs to, including family, body, clothes, and possessions. The social self is the person in relation to others, in any number of social roles. Each of us has many social selves, as we act differently in different social contexts – at work, with family members, with friends, and so on. The spiritual self is our core self, made up of our core values,

WEIGHING THE GHOST

In 1907, the American physician Duncan MacDougall (1866–1920) decided to measure the weight of the human soul. He devised a special bed that served also as a scale so that he could monitor the weight of his patients. He then selected six terminally ill patients who were going to die soon. He made sure each spent their last days in his weighing-bed and recorded their weight at regular intervals up to – and at the moment of – their death. From his data he calculated the weight of the soul to be 21 grams – the average weight loss of four of his patients at the point of death. It has since been shown that sloppy science accounted for the results – we still don't know whether there is a soul and, if there is, whether it has any mass (though it seems unlikely).

Is the soul a 'thing'?

beliefs, conscience and personality. It is the most fixed of the three, varying little during adult life.

James defined a person's 'Me' self as 'not only his body and his psychic powers, but his clothes and his house, his wife and children, his ancestors and friends, his reputation and works, his lands and horses, and yacht and bank-account' (1890). In claiming as 'mine' not only external objects but even other people ('my mother', even 'my enemy') he produced a diffuse, extended self that leaks into the environment – very much the opposite of the enclosed self of René Descartes that is distinct not just from others but even from its own body.

The 'I' self, which is pure ego, is the

According to William James, each of us has several 'social' selves.

stream of consciousness that provides an unbroken thread from the past through the present to the future. It also provides a sense of distinctness (contrasting with the appropriating 'Me' self) and of volition – it is responsible for choosing which thoughts to attend to and which to reject, so processing experience. The 'I' self is what we might think of as the mind or soul and, according to James, is not substance and so not susceptible to scientific examination.

Ghost gone again

Throughout much of the 20th century, psychology was dominated by a movement called behaviourism. This had no truck with the mind and placed all its emphasis on behaviour that could be observed. Most behaviourists were physical monists, paying attention only to the body. Some conceded the mind might exist, but as they had no way of accessing it and its processes directly, they felt that to all intents and purposes it might as well not exist at all.

When the mind resurfaced in the second half of the 20th century, neurology was snatching some of its traditional territory and passing it to the body.

We still can't locate or define consciousness, and the work of psychologists over the last 150 years has not brought consensus on the nature of the mind/body any closer. By the end of the Enlightenment, the full spectrum of models of how the mind and body might be divided or united was pretty much in place. The divisions that the ancient Greeks perceived within the mind are mirrored in the work of Freud and James. By the late 18th century, all the intellectual groundwork for psychology had been laid.

SIGISMUND SCHLOMO FREUD (1856–1939)

Freud was born in Příbor, Moravia (now in the Czech Republic) to poor Jewish parents. He was born with a caul – still covered by the amniotic membrane that forms the sac in which the foetus develops. His mother took this to be a good omen.

He studied medicine at the University of Vienna, then carried out research at the General Hospital in Vienna. In 1885 he became lecturer in neuropathology and went to Paris to study with Jean-Martin Charcot (1825–93), a neurologist researching hypnosis. It was a turning point in Freud's life. The following year, he resigned as lecturer and went into private practice, initially using hypnosis to get his patients to open up and reveal past traumatic experiences.

He soon realized he could forgo the hypnosis and he developed the technique of 'free association' (see page 203), in which he allowed patients to talk about whatever they wished, in any order. He began analysing dreams, which he felt gave him an insight into his patients' unconscious minds.

He saw all dreams as wish-fulfilment, subject to some censorship, but revealing our inner nature and most secret longings.

As Freud began to publish his theories and case studies, he developed a following. A group of disciples met with him once a week. Calling themselves 'the Wednesday Psychological Society', the group marked the beginning of the psychoanalytic movement. The Austrian music critic Max Graf (1873–1958), an early member of the group, recalled that, 'there was the atmosphere of the foundation of a religion in that room. Freud himself was its new prophet.'

But Freud was a Jew living in Vienna. For all his fame and prominence, after the Nazis came to power in Germany in 1933, Freud felt increasingly threatened. At a public bonfire of his writings, Freud commented, 'What progress we are making. In the Middle Ages they would have burned me. Now, they are content with burning my books.' He was finally persuaded (and helped) to leave Austria in 1939. He fled to London where he died the same year of jaw cancer – or, rather, of the overdose of morphine he asked his friend and physician Max Schur to administer.

CHAPTER 2

A body of **EVIDENCE:** measuring the mind

'How can one build up a science upon elements which, by very definition, are said to be private and noncommunicable?'

American psychologist Edward Tolman (1922)

Thinking, feeling, knowing, reasoning, learning, remembering, imagining – all these activities of the mind take place, wherever we choose to locate them. As objects of study, they are of enduring interest – yet they present unique problems to those who want to study them. The activities of the mind are individual and internal, so they are not susceptible to direct measurement or sharing. Even to study your own mind involves a tricksy recursiveness, for it is the mind studying itself. As Hume said, 'I can never catch myself at any time without a perception.' So how can the mind study itself? Bringing the methods of science and reason to bear on such a slippery subject has been an enduring challenge for psychologists.

Facing page: Meditation *by Henri Martin (1896).*

So – is psychology a science?

These very particular difficulties have led some thinkers to claim that psychology can never be a 'proper' science. The German philosopher Immanuel Kant (1724–1804), doubted there could ever be a 'science of the human mind'. He decided that it was most likely impossible, because its subject matter was subjective, internal, personal and incapable of external observation, testing or interrogation. A century later, the French positivist August Comte (1798–1857) rejected all knowledge except the publicly shareable observations of scientific enquiry. This meant that any kind of introspection was excluded, since it could be not shared for verification. And that meant that psychology was impossible:

'In order to observe, your intellect must pause from activity; yet it is this very activity you want to observe. If you cannot effect the pause you cannot observe; if you do effect it, there is nothing to observe. The results of such a method are in proportion to its absurdity. After two thousand years of psychological pursuit, no one proposition is established to the satisfaction of its followers. They are divided, to this day, into a multitude of schools, still disputing about the very elements of their doctrine...We ask in vain for any one discovery, great or small, which has been made under this method.'

Popper takes a pop at psychology

When Karl Popper became uncomfortable with the prevailing definition of science, he compared the theories of the physicist Albert Einstein with those of two psychologists, Sigmund Freud and his

How do we diagnose something that is subjective and intangible?

34

According to Karl Popper, in order to be scientific, a theory – such as Newton's movement of the planets – must have the potential to be proved wrong by alternative observations.

Austrian contemporary Alfred Adler (1870–1937). He realized that the significant difference is that Einstein's theory of relativity could be proved wrong by certain observations, while both Freud and Adler could interpret any new case according to their psychodynamic theories. Any and all new cases were framed by the two psychologists in such a way to fit, and so support, their theories.

To qualify as scientific, a theory must be capable of stating the observations that would cause it to be thrown out. For instance, Newton's theory of the movement of planetary bodies would have to be thrown out if we found a planet that followed a perfectly square path around its sun. How could Freud's theory of psychoanalysis be proved wrong? It can't – so it's not a scientific theory.

'A theory which is not refutable by any conceivable event is non-scientific. Irrefutability is not a virtue of a theory (as people often think) but a vice.'

With developments in other sciences, though, some aspects of mental activity did become capable of being measured and observed. Psychology emerged as that 'science of the human mind' that Kant doubted could exist, its quest to find definitive answers to some questions about the human mind and brain.

Semi-scientific

It seems that some aspects of psychology are scientific and some are not. Some ideas that in earlier times could never be tested – theories about which parts of the brain are used in different mental activities, for example – can now be examined using scientific methods such as brain scans. Other ideas – such as the theory that trauma in childhood might be responsible for criminal or neurotic behaviour in adulthood – still cannot be rigorously tested. For the moment, we probably have to accept psychology as sometimes scientific, and sometimes not. This chapter and the next will look at how the methods of experimentation have been applied to psychology. Necessarily, a lot of the work, particularly in earlier years, focused on the body, for the mind was – and to some degree still is – beyond the reach of empirical observers.

Ways of looking

People have thought about the activities of the mind for thousands of years. The first type of critical thinking about the mind was philosophical enquiry, and that continues to this day. Philosophy is a rigorous discipline that progresses through logic and structured argument to propose, refute, modify or endorse theories. It can tackle any subject and requires no tools apart from a brain and language – but it is not a science. The matter of philosophy is not susceptible to empirical proof or, as Popper would consider more important, to falsification.

Then, around the 16th century, as anatomists began to discover more about the human body and how it works, some scientists started to investigate how the brain and nervous system might work. Physiology, the study of bodily systems, offered a new approach to the mind and its interaction with the body, and one that provided new information and ideas for the philosophers.

A paradigm shift occurred in the mid-19th century when the English naturalist

An MRI scan can only tell us so much about the workings of the human mind.

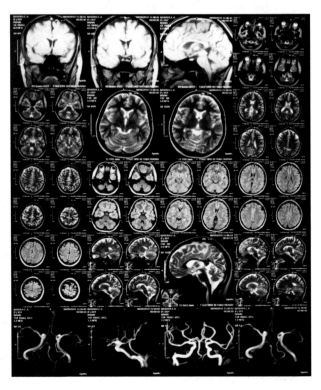

Charles Darwin (1809–82) proposed the theory of 'evolution by natural selection' in his seminal work *On the Origin of Species* (1859). This changed the way people thought about humanity's place in the world and the way they thought about science and knowledge. The distinction between humans and animals was no longer clear-cut: it could now only be called the differences

MONKEYANA.

AM I A MAN AND A BROTHER?

AM I satyr or man ?
Pray tell me who can,
And settle my place in the scale.
A man in ape's shape,
An anthropoid ape,

A satirical cartoon from 1861 responding to Charles Darwin's theory of evolution by natural selection.

between humans and other animals, and that made a lot of people uncomfortable. But if humans and animals were not so very different, perhaps useful information could be gathered from studying animal cognition and development. That made studies in comparative psychology – psychological

experiments on animals – a potentially useful tool in the exploration of the human mind. At much the same time, advances in technology meant that some mental processes could be measured, observed and recorded. Psychology emerged as a discrete discipline and psychologists began to approach the mind through experimentation. Twenty years after the publication of Darwin's *On the Origin of Species*, the first laboratory for experimental psychology was opened.

Child-as-guinea-pig

According to the Greek historian Herodotus (c.484–425BC), Psamtik I reigned as king of Egypt from 664–610BC. He has been credited with the first experiment in psychology. Hoping to discover the original and innate language of humans, he ordered two newborn babies to be given to a shepherd to care for, with strict instructions that no one should ever speak to them, or speak in their hearing. Psamtik hoped that the babies would begin talking by relying on innate knowledge of language. When one of the babies reportedly cried out 'bèkos', holding his arms outstretched, Psamtik took this to be the Phrygian word for bread and so proof that the Phrygian language was the language we were born to speak.

The forbidden experiment

The idea of raising children without language or even without any form of human contact has been named the 'forbidden experiment' as it is clearly highly unethical – yet its potential as a scientific tool is considerable. It has (reportedly) been tried on several occasions.

TYPES OF EXPERIMENT

Experimental methods aim to examine the relationship between variable conditions. There are two main types of variable. An independent variable is a condition that is manipulated by the researcher. A dependent variable is one that changes depending on the state of the independent variables. If you wanted to discover the temperature at which ice cream melts, you would examine it at different temperatures. Temperature is the independent variable, which you control. The solid/liquid state of the ice cream is the dependent variable, which changes as you change the temperature.

There are three types of experiment commonly used in psychological studies:

- Laboratory, or controlled, experiments: the experimenter has full control over the conditions and location of the experiment. It might be carried out with human subjects, animals or biological tissue, such as nerve cells.
- Field experiments: the experiment takes place in the everyday world. The experimenter has control over the important independent variables, but there will be other variables outside their control (such as the weather), making it hard to replicate an experiment later.
- Natural experiments: the experiment is really an observation of what happens in a real-world environment. The researcher has no control over variables. Natural experiments are not set up but rather the researcher notices the potential of a situation that could be studied. An example is the study of the development of children left in orphanages (see page 156).

In the 13th century, the Holy Roman Emperor Frederick II had infants raised without hearing human speech. The experiment was reported by the Italian friar and chronicler Salimbene di Adam (1221–90):

'Foster-mothers and nurses [were commanded] to suckle and bathe and wash the children, but in no ways to prattle or speak with them; for he would have learnt whether they would speak the Hebrew language (which had been the first), or Greek, or Latin, or Arabic, or perchance the tongue of their parents of whom they had been born. But he laboured in vain, for the children could not live without clappings of the hands, and gestures, and gladness of countenance, and blandishments.'

James IV of Scotland (reigned 1488–1513) sent two children to the remote island of Inchkeith to be raised by a mute woman. The children were reported to have begun to speak Hebrew, but the truth of this was doubted even at the time.

The Indian Mughal Emperor Akhbar the Great (reigned 1556–1605) believed that speech was not innate but acquired as children listened to others speaking. He isolated babies to discover whether children raised without speech would remain mute. It was reported that they developed a communication system based

Frederick II reputedly attempted the 'forbidden experiment' to discover what language God imparted to Adam and Eve.

on gesture, a finding supported by more recent observations of naturally occurring isolation.

The Indian emperor seems to be the only one who carried out the experiment from purely psychological curiosity rather than with a religious or political agenda.

Feral children

Of course, the forbidden experiment is only forbidden if set up by an experimenter. There have been several 'natural experiments' involving the observation of children who were raised outside normal society, either because they had been neglected or hidden away by abusive parents, or because they had been lost and raised by animals.

Stories of children brought up by animals date back thousands of years. Romulus reputedly overcame his unfortunate start in life – being brought up by a she wolf – to achieve greatness as founder and ruler of Rome. Most feral children are not so lucky (including Romulus' brother Remus). Although many earlier stories cannot be verified, reports from the 20th and 21st centuries include accounts of children brought up by dogs, wolves, monkeys, goats and even ostriches. One boy, found in India in 1979, was living an amphibious lifestyle near a river. Typically, feral children shows aspects of the lifestyle of the animals they have been raised with or by, eat raw food, shun human contact, often walk on all fours, and have no language skills (thereby refuting the reported results of some examples of the forbidden experiment).

'GENIE' (b.1957)

'Genie' was a victim of extreme abuse, kept locked alone in a room from the age of 20 months until she was 13 years old, when she was discovered by child welfare officers in Los Angeles. Her father had kept her tied up, unable to move more than her toes and fingers, had fed her only liquids and allowed no social contact. He had beaten her if she made a noise. When discovered, she could not walk, talk or eat solid food and was incontinent. She acquired rudimentary language skills and learned to walk, though with a strange stance. She was studied during attempts at rehabilitation until 1977 when her mother, blind and unable to look after Genie, refused any further scientific study of her. Her father shot himself before his trial for abuse. Genie currently lives in residential care in California and is non-verbal again.

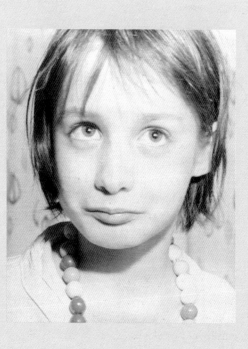

Children who have been kept secluded with animals behave in similar ways. A seven-year-old boy found in Russia in 2008 who had lived all his life in a room full of birds, and whose only human contact was his mother (who treated him like a bird), communicated by chirping and flapping his arms. All this evidence is useful data for the debate about how much of human activity (mental and physical) is due to heredity and how much to our home environment (see page 134 [Chapter 6: *Nature versus nurture*]).

Montaigne's first language was Latin.

In recent years, children who have been secluded or have lived in the wild and then been introduced into society have been closely observed during the process of their readjustment. Their terrible plight has provided rich pickings for psychologists.

Untold experiments

As it is so easy to 'experiment' with raising children, or with the treatment of employees or slaves (or women), it's likely that there have been many undocumented and probably unethical experiments born of everything from genuine scientific interest to idle or prurient curiosity. For example, the French essayist Michel de Montaigne (1533–92) was the subject of his father's experiments in child-rearing, being brought up to speak Latin as his first language and looked after for the first three years of his life by peasants rather than in his father's castle. On the whole, though, the recorded investigation of the human mind before the 19th century was achieved through philosophical enquiry.

41

Into the breach

The gap between philosophy and scientific psychology could only be bridged once some physiological knowledge was in place. That began during the 17th century, with the Scientific Revolution.

VITALISM V. MATERIALISM

Just as philosophy struggled with the mind/body problem, physiology wrestled with the issue of whether there was anything more to the body beyond the physical structures and processes. Vitalists maintained that there was a 'life force' that was something other than the physical body. As it was not physical, it was not amenable to investigation. The materialists, on the other hand, thought that there was nothing special about life and believed that humans, like any other organism, can be explained in terms of physical and chemical processes.

Getting on our nerves

The general idea that nerves carry information between the brain and parts of the body was not new – it is present even in the Greek philosopher Galen's accounts of physiology, written in the 2nd century AD. Neither Galen nor his successors were very clear about how the brain communicated with the body, but it seemed to involve some kind of moving 'spirits' travelling along the nerves, which were thought to be hollow. For 1,400 years, no one came up with a better idea.

'The Nerves are nothing else but productions of the marrowy and slimy substance of the Brain, through which the Animal spirits do rather beam than are transported. And this substance is indeed more fit for irradiation then a conspicuous or open cavity, which would have made our motions and sensations more sudden, commotive, violent and disturbed, whereas now the members receiving a gentle and successive illumination are better commanded by our will and moderated by our reason.'

Helkiah Crooke (1576–1648),
Microcosmographia, a Description of the Body of Man (1631)

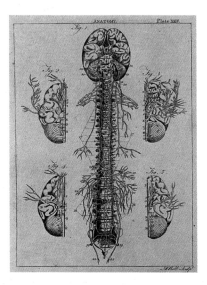

An 18th-century diagram of the nervous system.

Then, around 1630, René Descartes (see page 20) came up with a purely mechanical explanation in which the 'spirits' were replaced with fluid – a liquid, gas or 'fine flame' of some type. He still believed the nerves to be hollow, even though ten years previously Scottish medical student John Moir had recorded in his 1620 lecture notes: '…nerves have no perceptible cavity internally, as the veins and arteries have'.

Descartes gave the first precise explanation of how a reflex action might work. Any stimulus to a sense organ, he claimed, pulled the threads of the nerves taut and so opened a conduit in the corresponding part of the brain which allowed animal spirits to flow down the tubes to the affected area, swelling the muscles and causing them to move. Although he was wrong in all the details, the general principle is sound – a signal goes from the sensory nerves to the central nervous system, causing another signal to go to the motor nerves and move the muscles as necessary. He also suggested using the word 'stimulus' for that which excites the nerves.

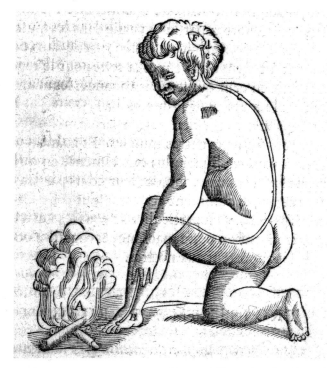

Descartes' illustration of a reflex action.

THE STATUES IN THE GARDEN

Descartes was inspired in his model of the nervous system by a series of automata in the gardens of St Germain, in France. These were moved by the flow of water through pipes, activated by people treading on pressure pads beneath the paths. Descartes thought that if statues could be moved in that way, maybe some similar mechanism was responsible for movement of the human body.

Descartes' work on the body was published after his death, in 1662. It was the only advance in theory relating to the nerves in 1,500 years, but his explanation was overturned just three years later by someone carrying out experimentation rather than thinking theoretically.

First of the frogs

In the 17th century, a young Dutch physiologist, Jan Swammerdam (1637–80), carried out experiments on frogs that showed that the brain rather than the heart was involved in movement but then, radically, demonstrated that movement could be induced even without the brain being present. He began by removing the heart and showing that the frog, though a mess, could still swim. When he removed the brain, it couldn't swim. But he showed that if he stimulated a nerve with his scalpel, a leg muscle would still contract. He could do the same with dogs. He could even make the muscle contract if the leg had been removed from the frog. Descartes' theory that spirits travelled from the brain to move the muscle mechanically was thoroughly disproven – the brain didn't even need to be in the same room.

Swammerdam's experiment was one of the most important in the history of neurophysiology and psychology. The connection he made between a stimulus and a response, carried out through the action of the nerves, laid the basis for behavioural psychology: the belief that the behaviour of an organism, human or other, is entirely the result of the sum total of all the stimuli it receives.

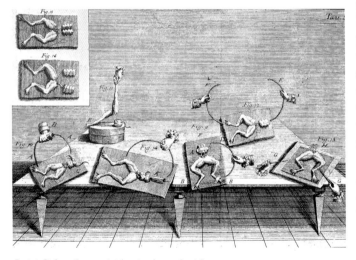

Luigi Galvani's experiments in electrophysiology.

Animal electricity

Although Swammerdam was certain that he had demonstrated that animal spirits don't

'*From these experiments, therefore, it may, I think, be fairly concluded, that a simple and natural motion or irritation of the nerve alone is necessary to produce muscular motion, whether it has its origin in the brain, or in the marrow, or elsewhere.*'
Jan Swammerdam (1678)

exist, he had not precisely explained how the nerves carry information. He likened it to vibrations travelling through a solid, such as a plank of wood, that has been knocked. The next step was taken by the Italian scientist Luigi Galvani (1737–98).

According to legend, Galvani was skinning a dead frog at a bench where he had previously been experimenting with static electricity when an assistant touched one of the frog's nerves with a metal scalpel. The leg made a jumping movement as though alive. Galvani went on to investigate the surprising result by passing electric currents through frog muscles and observing their movements. He concluded that 'animal electricity' was behind muscle movement in living things, and it was carried by the ionization of fluids in the body. There was still some work to do to put this together with the nerves, but he had made a startling discovery, the first in neurology.

Putting together the pieces

All that was left to do was to show how 'animal electricity' operates in the sensory and motor nerves and the brain. That occurred in 1811,

NON-ANIMAL ELECTRICITY
Repeating Galvani's experiments, the Italian physicist Alessandro Volta (1745–1827) recognized that the metal cable Galvani used to connect the muscles and nerves was passing the electric current between the two. Realizing the source of the electricity was biochemical, he set about reproducing the effect outside the body and developed the first battery. Applying electricity to frogs had thus kick-started two disciplines: neurology and electrical engineering.

when the British physiologist Charles Bell (1774–1842) produced a pamphlet outlining his findings from anatomical experiments with rabbits. Showing unusual compassion, Bell held off from carrying out his experiment for some time as he was concerned at the distress he must cause his subject by cutting through its nerves. In the end, he experimented on an unconscious rabbit.

'I therefore struck a rabbit behind the ear so as to deprive it of sensibility by the concussion, and then exposed the spinal marrow. On irritating the posterior roots of the nerve I could perceive no motion consequent on any part of the muscular frame; but on irritating the anterior roots of the nerve, at each touch of the forceps there was a corresponding motion of the muscles to which the nerve was distributed. These experiments satisfied me that the different roots and different columns from whence those roots arose were devoted to distinct offices, and that the notions drawn from the anatomy were correct.'

Charles Bell (1811)

Bell described different nerves for sensory and motor systems, connecting to the spinal cord at different places. The sensory nerves carry information from the sense organs, including sensory receptors in the skin, and enter the spinal column on the dorsal (back) side. The motor nerves connect at the ventral (front side) and carry information from the spinal column to the muscles. This confirmed that there is two-way traffic with signals going to

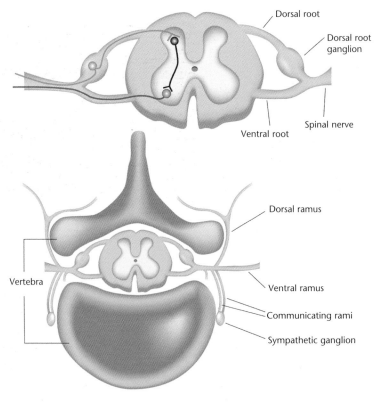

A cross section of the sensory and motor nerves connecting to the spinal cord.

and from the brain along different routes. Unfortunately, Bell did not publicize his discovery beyond producing a pamphlet he delivered to his friends. When the French physiologist François Magendie (1783–1855) made and published the same discovery eleven years later, dispute about priority ensued.

Bell suggested that there are five types of nerve, corresponding to our five senses, but it was left to the German physiologist Johannes Müller (1801–58) to demonstrate this. In 1835, he found that sensory nerves are particularly suited to specific types of stimulation (the eye works best with light, for example) but that they can also be

stimulated in other ways (we can experience visual hallucinations after a knock on the head, for example). He decided the specificity was in the nature of the nerve transmission rather than either the source of the stimulus or the area of the brain that processed the signal. (In that he was wrong; Lord Edgar

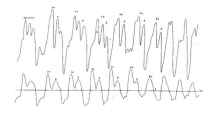

Johannes Müller's measurement of sensory response.

Adrian demonstrated in 1912 that the energy transmitted by all nerves is the same, it is where the signal comes from and how the brain processes it that varies.) Most importantly, though, his work demonstrated that our sense perceptions are determined internally – by the body and its nerves – not just by the nature of the external environment.

Sharks use a sense we don't have, electroreception, to locate their prey.

Towards a science of the mind

By the middle of the 19th century, the basic essentials of neuroscience had been discovered. In philosophy, there had been a move towards confidence in human achievement, confidence in science, and a belief that the world could be made better through the application of human ingenuity and knowledge. But we are getting ahead of ourselves. It was actually an exercise in astronomy that was the prompt for the first experiments in human psychology.

Sloppy work or a new science?

In 1795, the Astronomer Royal Nevil Maskelyne (1732–1811) and his assistant David Kinnebrooke were making astronomical calculations, by observing the point at which a star crossed a hairline in a telescope and timing it. Maskelyne chastised Kinnebrooke for being slow: his timings were consistently half a second slower than Maskelyne's. Eventually, when Kinnebrooke failed to improve his performance (indeed, it got worse), Maskelyne fired him and he went back to being a school teacher. It was twenty years before a German astronomer,

Friedrich Bessel (1784–1846), looked again at the results and wondered whether in fact Kinnebrooke was not being incompetent at all but whether there was a personal difference in response times. He carried out the first reaction-time study and calculated personal equations that enabled him to correct times between observers.

The German astronomer, Friedrich Bessel.

Bessel's study revealed that the observer influences observations, so that had to be taken into account with scientific observations of all types. He had also carried out the first psychology experiment into inter-personal differences. It was a field that would not gain much attention for a while, but would later become a massively important area of psychological research.

Psychophysics – getting physical with psychology

Measuring the speed of reactions was an early step in a new, quantitative approach to the physical aspects of psychology, called psychophysics. Psychophysics looks at the physical properties of stimuli and how they relate to perception. It has many applications in modern technology; in measuring the number of colours we can distinguish, for instance, it enables development of optimum compression algorithms for images.

Spot the difference

If a sound begins below the threshold of human hearing and steadily grows in volume, there comes a point at which you begin to notice it. Before that, the sound might have some subconscious effect on you, but you are not consciously aware of it. Similarly, if you pay attention to two slightly

different stimuli, there will be a point at which you can tell they are different. If they are too similar, however, you won't be able to tell them apart. The first person to try to quantify thresholds of perception was a German physician and one of the founders of experimental psychology, Ernst Heinrich Weber (1795–1878), working in Leipzig, Germany, in the 1830s.

Weber explored the degree of difference that people could detect in a stimulus, beginning with weights. He asked people to hold and compare different weights, reporting which was the heaviest. He found

When do you become aware of a noise, such as that made by a helicopter?

48

that there must be a difference of 3 per cent between weights for people to be able to tell them apart – for there to be a 'just noticeable difference', or JND. So, if one weight was 100 grams, a second would need to be 3 grams lighter or heavier to be detectably different. If one weighed a kilogram, the second would need to be 30 grams heavier or lighter to be perceived as different, and so on. He found different degrees applied to different senses, so in comparing the lengths of two lines, for example, there must be a difference of at least 1 per cent; a comparison of musical pitches, on the other hand, requires a difference of at least 0.6 per cent, and so on.

Weber's law states that:

$$\Delta R / R = k$$

where:

ΔR = the smallest detectable stimulus (or JND)
R = amount of existing stimulation (from *Reiz* in German)
K = a constant (different for each sense)

He studied other aspects of thresholds of perception, too. Using compass points, he measured the distance between two touches on the skin that could be separately discerned, and the point at which a sensation could not be detected at all. It was a landmark in the history of psychology, for it showed that at least some aspects of the subject could be studied by quantitative scientific methods. It laid the foundations for the acceptance of experimental psychology as a field of study.

Gustav Fechner, c.1870.

Crossing the threshold

Weber's work was continued by Gustav Fechner (1801–87), who had trained first as a physicist but had to resign his professorship after suffering eye damage while investigating colour and vision. He transferred his interest to the psychological process of perception. A neutral monist, he considered bodily and conscious acts to be different aspects of a single reality and set about finding a mathematical relationship between them. He wanted to solve the mind-body problem in a way that would satisfy the materialists but also endorse his own view that consciousness was everywhere in the universe.

Fechner defined the point at which a stimulus becomes noticeable as the 'absolute threshold'. Below this point, a stimulus

Ernst Heinrich Weber.

might still have an effect, but it would be an unconscious one. As this couldn't be measured, he started from the absolute threshold. His work resulted in the Weber–Fechner law, a refined version of Weber's conclusion:

'In order that the intensity of a sensation may increase in arithmetical progression, the stimulus must increase in geometrical progression.'

This means that there is a logarithmic relationship between the intensity of a stimulus and the intensity of the resulting sensation. (Logarithmic scales are used to measure very wide variations in related phenomena, such as the Richter scale for earthquakes or the decibel measure of sound.)

Where S is sensation and R is stimulus:

$$S = k \log R$$

Suppose that we find that tripling the intensity of a stimulus doubles the intensity of a sensation. If we then tripled the intensity of the stimulus again, the intensity of the sensation would increase by the same amount as previously, now it would be triple the original (even though the intensity of the stimulus is now nine times the original). Tripling the stimulus yet again makes the sensation four times the original – and so on.

Fechner felt he had achieved his aim: he had shown a measurable link between physical stimuli and a response in the psyche. Modern findings do not entirely match Fechner's 'law'.

His work, published in 1860 as *Elements of Psychophysics*, was an early attempt to use quantitative scientific methods to investigate psychological phenomena. Some commentators have seen it as marking the beginning of psychology as a science. For others, that distinction goes to Wilhelm Wundt's founding of the first laboratory for experimental psychology (see page 56 [Chapter 3: *Wundt's wonderful invention*]).

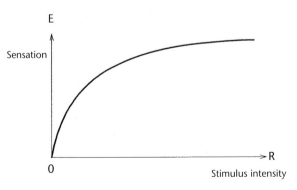

WEBER-FECHNER'S LAW

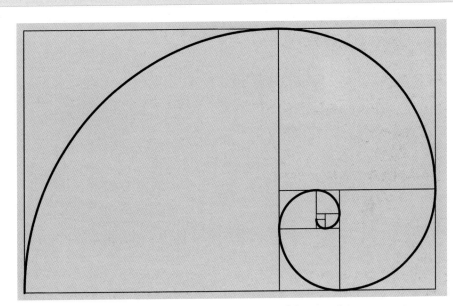

A 'golden spiral', created by drawing circular arcs in the tiles of the rectangle.

GOLDEN RECTANGLES AND SPLIT CONSCIOUSNESS

Amongst his other work, Fechner conducted a study on aesthetically pleasing shapes and discovered that people found a rectangle with sides in the proportion 0.62 to be the most attractive. This corresponds to the golden ratio and the Fibonacci sequence, found everywhere in nature from the pattern in the seeds of a sunflower to the proportions of a nautilus shell. He also proposed that if a brain could be split along the corpus callosum – a band of fibres that joins the two hemispheres – it would be possible to have two independent streams of consciousness. Fechner doubted such an experiment could ever be conducted, but the neuropsychologist Roger Sperry (1913–94) and psychologist Michael Gazzaniga (b.1939), found that Fechner was correct while working in the 1960s with epileptic patients whose corpus callosum had been severed to treat their condition.

AKA DR MISES

Fechner published several pamphlets or articles that presented his panpsychic views and satirized aspects of the prevailing orthodoxy. As these views would have undermined his reputation as a serious scientist, he presented them under the name Dr Mises. They included titles such as *The Comparative Anatomy of Angels* (1825) and *A Little Book of Life After Death* (1836).

Measuring the speed of thought

The German physician and physicist Hermann von Helmholtz (1821–94) was the first to make a serious attempt at measuring the speed of nerve impulses. He began with the ever-useful frogs and progressed to humans, finding that the response time depended on how far the impulse had to travel. In 1849, he carried out experiments in which he stimulated a subject's leg and asked the person to press a button when they felt it. The reaction took longer when he stimulated the toe than when he stimulated the thigh. He concluded that in humans the speed is 27 metres per second. In fact, the fastest human nerve transmission is faster than a racing car, at 430 kilometres per hour (or 110 metres per second), though others can be much slower, down to around 50 metres per second. More important than the rather variable speeds he measured was the fact that he demonstrated there is a speed: many people believed that transmission was instantaneous, especially those who gave to God the task of realizing intention as action.

Helmholtz's pendulum, used to measure the speed of a nerve impulse. The swing of the pendulum stimulates a nerve in a muscle.

Helmholtz was also interested in Müller's findings that the sense organs can only produce their 'own' type of perception, so (for instance) a blow to the eye makes us 'see' stars. Because all the eye/brain link can do with information from the eyes is to make visual images, that's what it does, even when that's not the most appropriate response. Helmholtz wanted to know why and how this happened and set out – ambitiously – to trace all the physiological processes involved from the moment a sensory nerve is stimulated to the point at which the sensation is recognized. It is a task that still has not been achieved.

came the task requiring discrimination between stimuli, while the task requiring discrimination and choice was slowest. He calculated the time taken to discriminate, and the time taken to choose and respond – measurements of activity taking place entirely within the brain.

With Donders' experiment, it became possible to infer activity inside the brain (or mind) from experimental data. The stage was set for experimental psychology. The first person to step on to that stage was Wilhelm Wundt.

Franciscus Donders.

Moving inside

Fifteen years later, the Dutch physiologist Franciscus Donders (1818–89) decided to make more complex measurements of reaction times. As well as timing how long it took a subject to respond to a stimulus, he added complications. First, he used a selection of stimuli and asked the subject to respond only to one of them, while ignoring the others. Next, he used a selection of stimuli and required a different response for each. Subjects had to identify the stimulus and make the right response. He found the simple stimulus/response task was the quickest, then

CHAPTER 3

Mind and
METHOD:
how and why do we think?

'Materialist psychology…is contradicted by the fact of consciousness itself, which cannot possibly be derived from any physical qualities of material molecules or atoms.'

Wilhelm Wundt (1912)

To many people today, the idea of psychology is perhaps most familiar through the image of the psychotherapist analysing a patient, or an experiment investigating the behaviour of people or rats. From this starting point, the earliest psychology experiments would look rather alien, and perhaps rather barren. But they formed the stepping stones to some of the most famous psychological experiments of the 20th century, some of which challenged and rewrote the way we see ourselves as humans.

Facing page: *A 15th-century diagram of consciousness.*

Wundt's wonderful invention

Wundt set out to understand consciousness and the mental laws that govern it. At the heart of his approach was the concept of will – of the individual's choice of what to attend to and so what to perceive. He called his branch of psychology 'voluntarism' because the voluntary aspect was vital to him, though his approach later grew to be associated with structuralism (which was really an outgrowth of his methods). Wundt set out to achieve this goal by experimenting with human subjects, and set up the first experimental psychology laboratory in the world to carry out his work.

In investigating consciousness, Wundt aimed to discover the basic elements of thought, and then to discover the laws that governed their combination. His approach was through introspection, which required subjects to observe and report their own internal state. His experiments involved using various types of equipment to produce stimuli and measure reaction times, or asking subjects to reflect carefully on and report their response to a stimulus such as a light or a ticking metronome. From their reports he tried to unpick the elements of consciousness.

His account (and what he required of his subjects) looks highly technical and complex. When a person experiences a stimulus there is a corresponding sensation. According to Wundt, the sensation can be broken down into modality (type – such as vision, or taste) and intensity. Sensations are accompanied by feelings. These can be described in terms of three axes:

- pleasant/unpleasant
- excitement/calmness
- strain/relaxation.

These are not usually experienced in isolation. The combination of feelings

WILHELM WUNDT (1832–1920)

Wundt was born into a family of middle-class intellectuals in Mannheim, Germany. With his one surviving brother sent away to school, Wundt grew up without companions of his own age (save for one mentally impaired boy who could barely speak). Although not a promising student at school, he went on to excel in his study of medicine. He switched his attention to psychology in 1855. The following year, he returned to Heidelberg and worked as Hermann Helmholtz's assistant and began teaching a course in psychology. Although he wanted to teach experimental psychology, the university would not give him laboratory space until 1879. Once he had set up his lab, however, he immediately attracted students from all around Europe. His lectures were the most popular in the university, but still the university did not welcome his work and his Institute for Experimental Psychology was not listed in its catalogue until 1883. Even so, his Institute grew, being rehoused several times until it was given its own building in 1897.

Wundt finished work on his autobiography a few days before his death, making it as complete as an autobiography can be.

experienced together produces perception. It is a passive process, produced by the combination of the stimulus acting on the person to produce sensations and feelings that depend upon the individual's past history, personal physiology and so on. We are not entirely governed by this passive process, though. Within the sensations and feelings produced, we choose which elements to pay attention to, and those form our 'apperceptions'.

This is how Wundt's model works. Suppose you visit a café with two other people. For you the strong smell of croissants brings back pleasant memories of a holiday in France. For someone else, the same smell will trigger different personal reflections – perhaps they were given some bad news while eating fresh croissants and now the aroma has unhappy associations. For the third person, the smell is neither here nor there – it's just a smell. You are all exposed to the same physical stimulus. Your experience of sensation is the same, but the feelings that are produced are not.

Wundt would vary the speed of a metronome and ask his subjects to record their responses to the noise.

Your perceptions and apperceptions are different. You might revel in the smell and rejoice in the pleasant memories. The second person might try to blot out the experiences that the smell recalls. The third person does not have it as part of their current apperception at all.

Reaching the limit

Wundt thought that although introspection could unravel the basic thought elements, helping us to understand consciousness and what is going on in the mind at any particular moment, higher mental processes are beyond this type of analysis. He believed that psychological processes, like physical processes, are subject to specific laws, but that these laws were so complex, depending on so many unmeasurable and unobservable factors, that prediction is impossible.

Even though Wundt believed we can't predict what will happen in the mind, he thought that after the event we can sometimes unpick what has happened and explain it, and even see its inevitability. This looking-backwards approach would later become fundamental to psychoanalysis.

Wundt's work was important primarily in establishing that experimental psychology was a viable proposition. Later critics objected that although he applied scientific rigour to the methods of experimentation, introspection can never be a valid scientific tool as it is incapable of being measured or observed objectively. The later behaviourists (see below) avoided this problem by working with measurable behaviours and refusing to probe the mental acts that produce them. Even so, Wundt's interest in thoughts and consciousness prepared the ground for the cognitive psychology that emerged in the second half of the 20th century.

Structuralism

The large number of students who flocked to Wundt's laboratory soon came from as far afield as the USA, and many went on to found psychology departments in other universities. One of these was in Cornell University in New York and was run by a newly-graduated doctoral student of Wundt's, Edward Titchener (1867–1927).

While Wundt wanted to explain the mind and its mental processes, Titchener only wanted to describe them with scientific precision. He felt that explanation was beyond the realm of science, and his brand of experimental psychology was thoroughly scientific. He called his approach 'structuralism', as he sought to investigate the structure of the mind. His interests lay only in consciousness, with no regard to the unconscious mind or instincts.

Titchener developed Wundt's ideas of introspection and mental elements, but his versions were considerably changed. Instead of just noting whether they did or did not respond to a stimulus, Titchener's subjects were asked to observe their response and describe it in elemental terms, breaking it down as far as possible. Rather than naming an object presented to them, for instance, subjects had to report the sensations they received – describing the object as warm, heavy, red, and so on.

Titchener determined that the elements of consciousness are 'sensations' (elements of perceptions), 'images' (elements of ideas) and 'affections' (elements of emotions). He distinguished more than 40,000 sensations, most of them relating to sight. Studying sensations took up most of his time. He measured them in terms of quality, duration, intensity, clearness and 'extensivity' (to what degree a sensation extended over an area or space). The same attributes applied to ideas. For emotions, the only meaningful attribute was pleasantness/unpleasantness.

He believed all previous experiences come into play when we give sense to something. This is based on association – the action of the mind making associations between experiences that occur close together, or that are frequently encountered together (see page 96). Titchener rejected Wundt's theory of apperception.

For all its detailed structure and focus on scientific rigour – in part, because of them – Titchener's approach did not survive his death. It left out too much that was becoming important in psychology, and its reliance on introspection was itself problematic. Some critics pointed out that

Edward Titchener, c.1917.

it was really retrospection, as the mental event had happened by the time the subject described it. The account of introspection was impure: it was tainted or distorted by memory, and even by the act of looking at it. The type of objective scientific method that Titchener wanted to use to explore psychology didn't really seem to work after all, at least not when applied in this way.

Functionalism

At the same time that Titchener was developing his structural approach to the mind, one of the most influential American psychologists, William James (1842–1910), was developing a different approach. 'Functionalism' focused not on the static structure of the mind, but on the function or purpose of mental processes. It related the activity of the mind to Darwinian evolution and took a more holistic, integrated approach: how did the mind work to help the individual survive?

Functionalism and evolution

The functionalist school of psychology developed from the theory of evolution. The central tenet of functionalism was that the actions of the mind have a function and this function has served to make the organism better suited to its environment and the life it must live.

WILLIAM JAMES (1842–1910)

Born into a wealthy and influential New York family, James was exposed to the ideas of many great thinkers of the day. James' education took place partly in the USA and partly in Europe, and he became fluent in French and German. At first he wanted to be an artist, but his father so disapproved that James changed his mind and decided to train in science, enrolling at Harvard in 1861. In 1864 he transferred to Harvard's medical school. Although he qualified as a medical doctor, he never practised medicine.

In early adult life, James suffered several forms of physical illness (he had to abandon an Amazonian expedition with the Swiss naturalist Louis Agassiz because of seasickness and smallpox) as well as psychological symptoms, including depression. His depression was eventually alleviated by finding a philosophical position that provided meaning for him.

He remained at Harvard for the rest of his life, establishing psychology as a field of study there and setting up the first teaching laboratory in the subject anywhere in the world. His students included the US president Theodore Roosevelt, the Spanish philosopher George Santayana and the American novelist Gertrude Stein.

After publishing his seminal work, *Principles in Psychology* (1890), James wanted to move away from experimental psychology to concentrate more on philosophy and his interest in psychic phenomena. He helped found the American Society for Psychical Research in 1884.

A self-portrait from William James' notebook, drawn at the time of his ill-fated Amazonian expedition.

As the name suggests, functionalism was concerned with the functioning of the mind. It did not study the mind as a static object, but was interested in it in action and in what its action is for. Instead of looking only at the mainstream – the psychology of normal, adult humans – functionalism also took in animal behaviour, child psychology and abnormal psychology. As the environment for each person is different, what makes one person suited to their environment is not necessarily the same as makes another person suited to theirs – such as patience in a driving instructor or competitiveness in a stock broker. Consequently, functionalism was as concerned with differences between people as with the common ground they share.

Right: *Ideally, the emerging mind develops to suit the individual to their environment and needs.*

PUTTING IT TO USE

Functionalism, being concerned with how and why the mind works as it does, has a clear interest in the uses of mental processes and behaviours. The functionalists were interested in psychology as a practical science with useful applications, rather than as a pure science – knowledge for its own sake. In functionalism, we find the origins of the applications that attempt to use psychology to make people's lives better: improving education, work and the treatment of the sick, for example. Intelligence testing became an important strand in applied psychology during the early 20th century. Functionalism, then, was broadly pragmatic – a point of clear distinction from the structuralists who avoided any practical application of psychological knowledge.

The birth of American psychology

The publication of *Principles of Psychology* (1890) by William James marked the point at which American psychology broke away from philosophy and from European traditions in psychology. The brother of the novelist Henry James, William taught at Harvard where he set up a teaching laboratory in 1875. Wundt's laboratory, though established four years later, is generally considered the first as it was experimental, whereas James' was used exclusively for demonstrations. Running to nearly 1,400 pages, the *Principles* set out a view in opposition to Wundt's.

James popularized the phrase 'stream of consciousness'. He believed that consciousness was continuous, from birth to death, was constantly changing and so could not be divided or stopped for psychologists to take a look at it. The 'elements of consciousness' approach taken by Wundt was, then, meaningless in James' view. Further, the importance of consciousness for the individual is that it aids survival. It chooses which things to attend to, and they would be the things useful to the individual.

James considered that both instincts and habits are behaviours useful to the organism, whether animals or human beings. Habits, he believed, are behaviours that have been reinforced during the course of the individual's life. By repetition, they become entrenched and are then less costly in terms of conscious effort.

'Consciousness, then, does not appear to itself chopped up in bits. Such words as "chain" or "train" do not describe it fitly as it presents itself in the first instance. It is nothing jointed; it flows. A "river" or "stream" are the metaphors by which it is most naturally described. In talking of it hereafter, let us call it the stream of thought, of consciousness, or of subjective life.'

William James (1890)

James initially struggled with the concept of free will. As a young man, he was thrown into despair by the determinism he saw as the inevitable consequence of accepting the theory of evolution. If the materialist view of psychology that he had learned in Germany was correct, then everything that a human did was an inevitable consequence of neurophysiology as it had developed over the course of evolution. There was, then, no freedom in human action, and no hope or choice in life. He was saved from depression by reading an essay by the French philosopher Charles Renouvier (1815–1903), which persuaded him that he might freely choose to attend to one thought rather than another when several were available to him.

This inspiration had a significant impact on his later psychological theories. He decided that in choosing which thoughts to attend to, we determine both our personalities and the actions we take. The actions we take determine how we feel – this is counterintuitive as we usually suppose that our actions stem from how we feel. Suppose you saw a bear approach you in the woods and you ran away. You might think that you ran away because you were frightened – but James said that you were frightened because you ran away. The body acts instinctively to run away from the dangerous bear and the brain interprets the running away as signalling fear, so you feel frightened. His advice to act in the way you wish to feel stems from his belief that our emotions take their cues from our behaviour. Consequently, if you are miserable, smiling in spite of your misery will eventually cheer you up. Experiments carried out later in the 20th century by social psychologists Leon Festinger and James Merrill Carlsmith exploring cognitive dissonance (see page 157–158 [Chapter 6: *Becoming yourself*]) seem to support James' view.

James was highly influential, but had little interest in experimentation so did not contribute much to developing methodology.

The rise of pragmatism

In his later years, James became increasingly interested in parapsychology and sought a replacement for his work at Harvard so that he could focus on his work in psychic phenomena. He was succeeded by Hugo Münsterberg (1863–1916), a German-born psychologist who was deeply unimpressed by James' forays into mysticism, parapsychology and the newly emerging psychoanalysis. He felt these had no place in psychology, which he considered an eminently practical science. Indeed, he completely dismissed the unconscious that was central to psychoanalysis and to James' parapsychology interests. Münsterberg's work focused on aspects of psychology that would be of practical use in the world, initiating the fields of forensic psychology (which applies psychology to criminality) and industrial psychology (applying it to the workplace).

Münsterberg was the first to consider how psychology could be applied to legal cases, arguing that brutal interrogation of criminals would not yield useful results as it would lead suspects to give unreliable accounts. For example, they might say what they think the interrogator wants to hear, rather than the truth, in order to end the questioning, or they might be innocent and yet lie in order to seek punishment because of underlying depressive issues. He outlined a design for a device that would uncover lying by measuring physiological changes such as altered pulse or rate of breathing – a train of thought that would eventually lead to the development of the lie detector.

Functionalism comes of age

The American philosopher and psychologist John Dewey (1859–1952) developed functionalism and pragmatism in new directions, though he called his version of psychology 'instrumentalism'. First a teacher and then a philosopher, Dewey brought to psychology a strong interest in pedagogy. Following James' lead, he considered that dividing consciousness into stages was invalid, but extended this also to dividing behaviour into elements. He did

Hugo Münsterberg.

not find the common way of considering a reflex action in three parts – sensory process, brain process, motor process – a useful approach, since it doesn't take account of the integrated nature of an experience. Using the example of a child touching a flame, feeling pain, and withdrawing, he pointed out that the most important part of the sequence is that the child learns that flames hurt and their future behaviour is modified by this knowledge. This is an outcome the usual account ignores because it stops with the withdrawal of the hand.

Dewey saw the adaptive function of

A murder suspect takes a lie detector test, c.1954.

> 'The story of the subconscious mind can be told in three words: there is none.'
>
> Hugo Münsterberg (1909)

experience as vital, and considered that all behaviour should be viewed in this way – in terms of its function in helping the individual adapt to their environment. The adaptation was to make the organism more fit to survive.

A liberal who believed that all philosophy and psychology must have practical applications, Dewey supported women's suffrage, liberal democracy, the rights of black people, intellectual freedom and progressive education. He also directed the Dewey Commission held in Mexico in 1937 that found Leon Trotsky innocent of the crimes he was accused of by Stalin.

In 1906, James Rowland Angell (1869–1949) took over from Dewey as president of the American Psychological Association. The functional psychologist, he said, is interested in 'mental activity as part of a larger stream of biological forces'. As such, functional psychologists aligned themselves with evolutionary biology; they saw mental processes aiding in adaptation, and helping the organism to survive.

John Dewey presents birth control activist and nurse, Margaret Sanger, with an American Women's Association medal in 1932.

The mind and body are an inseparable unit, working together for the survival of the organism. The strong link with evolutionary theory led functionalists to embrace animal behaviour and child psychology as useful tools. They retained introspection, but added a multitude of experimental techniques to the psychologist's toolbox.

The adaptive act

The American psychologist Harvey Carr (1873–1954) explained the 'adaptive act' at the heart of the functionalist approach to behaviour. It comprises three components: first, a motive acts as a stimulus (such as thirst, or the need to escape danger); second, there is a specific environmental setting; and third, a response satisfies the motivating need. The environment is important as it affects the need – seeing a bear in a zoo is not at all the same thing as seeing a bear when you are walking in the woods. The organism learns that the behaviour has satisfied the need, and will resort to it again when the same need arises, hence the act is adaptive, helping the organism to survive with minimal effort. This is the last, meaningful, part of the child-burned-by-fire jigsaw.

Psychoanalysis and the psychodynamic approach

At much the same time as functionalism emerged in the United States, a new movement in Europe rejected the objective approach altogether. In a consulting room in Vienna, Sigmund Freud was developing the process of psychoanalysis, and putting together his theories about the unconscious mind and how early experiences determine character. Freud's approach began as a therapeutic endeavour to help patients suffering mental distress but it soon developed into a theory about the structure and working of the mind. His methods were entirely subjective, involving in-depth conversations, or analysis, with individuals. His theories are based primarily on case studies. This approach has clear

In functionalist theory, the environment is central to defining our behavioural responses.

shortcomings in that he was deriving his ideas about the mind in general not just from a small sample of similar people (middle-class, 19th-century citizens of Vienna) but also exclusively on people who already felt they were suffering from mental distress.

Psychoanalysis was not the only psychodynamic method. Alfred Adler (1870–1937) developed a competing method, called 'Individual Psychology'. Like Freud, he believed that actions and mental states are determined by earlier experiences. Whereas Freud saw sexuality and the sexual drive as central, Adler saw the 'inferiority complex' as the most important element in determining adult character, problems and behaviour. All psychodynamic approaches are highly deterministic: they make events and influences early in life responsible for what happens to a person later, robbing the individual of agency.

The third International Psychoanalytic Conference, held at Weimar in 1911. Among the attendees pictured are Freud, Carl Jung and Otto Rank.

The indivisible whole

Throughout the 1890s and early 1900s, psychology was dominated by polar opposite approaches – the psychodynamic and functionalist schools – one on each side of the Atlantic. Then, at almost the same time, two new movements in psychology emerged. Both took the problems with structuralism and functionalism as their starting points. One of these was Gestalt psychology, from the German *gestalt*, or 'whole'. The other was behaviourism.

Gestalt psychology rejected the idea of breaking consciousness or stimuli and responses into constituent elements and the inevitable fragmentation of experience that resulted from this. The Gestaltists claimed that this is not how we experience the world; the conscious experience is felt and must be studied as a unified whole. We don't see the parts of a dog and piece them together to understand that there is a dog present – we recognize what we see and hear as a dog all in one go. The Gestaltists concentrated on phenomena – entire, experienced, internal or external events and behaviours. They demonstrated this using experimental methods.

Seeing the light

The origins of Gestalt psychology are generally credited to an Austro–Hungarian psychologist, Max Wertheimer (1880–1943), on a train journey between Vienna and the Rhineland in 1910. Having an idea about the nature of perception, he got off the train at Frankfurt and bought a toy stroboscope, which flashed a sequence of still images in rapid succession to give the impression of a moving image. In his Frankfurt hotel room, he experimented with how the speed of perceiving a sequence of images can produce the perception of movement, though not the movement that is actually happening (that is, movement of the stroboscope).

Later, in his laboratory, Wertheimer experimented with equipment that could

A phenakistoscope uses a spinning disc to create the illusion of movement.

flash lights on and off at differing speeds. He found that by varying the speed of two alternately flashing lights he could produce the perception that there was one light that was permanently on, or was flashing on and off, or was moving between two points (this last is called the 'phi phenomenon'). The eyes, then, can lie: what we perceive is not necessarily what we see. The principle of Gestalt psychology was to begin with the perceived event or experience and work from the top down to determine what produced it and how, not to work from the bottom up, gathering what were believed to be the components of perception or experience and building with them.

Wertheimer worked closely with the German psychologists Kurt Koffka (1886–1941) and Wolfgang Köhler (1887–1967), who were originally his test subjects for the phi phenomenon experiments. The three are often cited as joint originators of Gestalt psychology.

The circle and the melody

The Austrian philosopher Christian von Ehrenfels (1859–1932) discussed the relationship between the elements of a sensory perception and our understanding of the whole experience. For example, he described the way in which we experience a melody in its entirety rather than attending to the individual notes. If the melody is transposed into a different key we still perceive it as the same melody, even though the individual notes are different. (The same notes could also be reused in a different melody.) This he called the *Gestalt-qualität*, which means something like 'quality of wholeness', and which we add somehow in the act of perception.

Wertheimer was a pupil of Ehrenfels and was inspired by him. He went further, saying, 'What is given me by the melody does not arise…as a secondary process from the sum of the pieces as such. Instead, what takes place in each single part already depends upon what the whole is.' So we first hear the melody and only afterwards might divide it up into notes. He found an example in vision, too. If we see a circle, we see it first in its entirety as a circle and only afterwards notice how it is made up. We see the circle 'im-mediately' – that is, not mediated by a process of adding together the parts.

Wolfgang Köhler's research into the problem-solving abilities of apes has been seen as a turning point in the psychology of thinking.

GESTALT SPY: HAS MONKEYS, WILL TRAVEL

In 1913, the German psychologist Wolfgang Köhler (1887–1967) went to Tenerife in the Canary Islands to study chimpanzees. He was to stay there for seven years. There has been speculation, reinforced by reports from two of his children and the man who looked after his experimental animals, that during the First World War Köhler spied for the Germans. With a concealed radio, he is said to have notified the German Navy of any Royal Navy activity in the area. Once the coast was clear, German ships were able to enter the area to refuel. Köhler did actually carry out the research on chimpanzees he was officially engaged in, however. His devotion to Germany did not survive the rise of Nazism: after speaking out against the persecution of the Jews, he left Germany for good in 1935 to live and work in the USA.

How it works

Wertheimer and the Gestaltists proposed a mechanism by which sensory impressions are transformed by the mind into whole perceptions. The mind, they claimed, has pre-existing electrochemical fields that act on incoming sense perceptions in a way comparable with a magnetic field acting on iron particles. From the interaction of sensory data with force-fields in the brain, fields of mental activity result that form into configurations that are experienced as perception.

The Law of Precision

According to Gestalt psychology, the brain will always tend towards an interpretation that is as simple, symmetrical and well organized as circumstances allow. This can be demonstrated experimentally by showing people various images and asking what they see. The Gestaltists found that when we look at a figure, we try to recognize in it some kind of order. So if we look at this:

We organize it into an overlapping triangle and square – we don't see a jumble of lines and angles. This they called the law of Prägnanz ('precision'). It has given rise to several laws of Gestalt that explain how we organize visual perception to create order from apparent chaos.

The law of proximity leads us to see objects in close proximity as groups. We see these circles as three groups of 12 rather than 36 discrete circles:

The law of similarity leads us to group things if they are similar. Here we see three rows of white circles and three rows of black circles, rather than just a block of 36 circles:

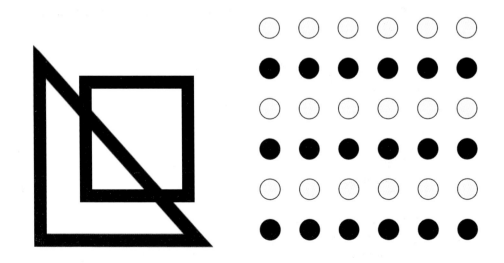

The law of symmetry makes us group objects by physical similarity. So we see this figure as three sets of symmetrical brackets, not six separate brackets or two single brackets and two mismatched pairs:

[ ] { } [ ]

The law of past experience can over-rule the other laws. It draws on what we already know to help us interpret what we see. If we are reading text and come across 'OO' we are likely to interpret this as letters – double 'o' – but if we are looking at a page of figures we are more likely to see this as a number – double zero.

The law of common fate makes us group objects if they move together or in the same direction, like the birds above.

The law of continuity is what makes you see these images as two lines that cross rather than four lines that meet:

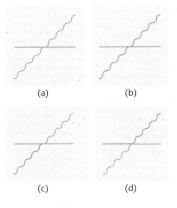

(a) (b)

(c) (d)

The law of closure leads us to see completed, anticipated shapes. So we will consider the figure below to be a circle with a broken outline, not a series of curved lines.

The law of 'good Gestalt' says that we perceive shapes and lines together if they form an object that is simple, regular and concise. We see the figure on page 70 as a square and a triangle overlapping or joined, not an irregular shape with eight sides.

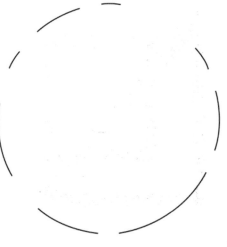

The principles underlying how our brains create meaning out of what we see are, in Gestalt terms, 'reification', 'emergence', 'multistability' and 'invariance':

- Multistability stems from a confusion between the background and foreground of an image. When it seems that part of a picture could be either foreground or background, our minds switch frantically between the two, as in the famous Rubin vase, below: is it a vase or two faces?
- Invariance is our ability to recognize an

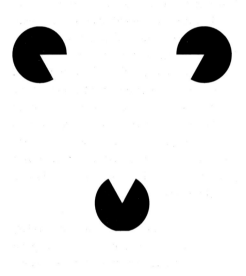

- Reification is the tendency to see a recognizable object even when it is not really there. The picture above, for instance, leads us to see a complete shape – a white triangle – rather than three black circles with sections cut out.
- Emergence is the tendency to see a recognizable image in an abstract pattern of lines or shapes. For example, you may be able to see a Dalmatian dog in the picture on the right.

Once you've recognized the dog, it's then hard to 'unsee' it. It's also the phenomenon behind the toast, teacakes, clouds, or coffee froth that seem to show the image of Christ or the name of Allah.

object as being the same, even after it has been rotated, inverted, seen at a distance, cast in shadow or otherwise seemingly altered.

Gestalt psychology is not concerned with explaining how these features of perception come about but only recognizing that they do and that this governs how we perceive the world.

Nazism cost Germany the Gestalt movement as, by 1935, all its major protagonists had left to live in the USA. Gestalt psychology is no longer evident as a strand on its own, but a lot of its thinking has been absorbed into other schools of psychology.

Behaving as yourself

In 1913, the year after Wertheimer set out on the path to Gestalt, John B. Watson (1878–1958), on the other side of the Atlantic, came out of the closet as a behaviourist. In an influential lecture, 'Psychology as the Behaviorist Views It', he went fully public with behaviourist tendencies. Previously, his ideas had been met with criticism and he had retreated. With the 1913 lecture there was no turning back: behaviourism was here to stay. In his opening remarks he set out his stall:

'Psychology as the behaviorist views it is a purely objective experimental branch of natural science. Its theoretical goal is the prediction and control of behavior. Introspection forms no essential part of its methods, nor is the scientific value of its data dependent upon the readiness with which they lend themselves to interpretation in terms of consciousness. The behaviorist,

in his efforts to get a unitary scheme of animal response, recognizes no dividing line between man and brute. The behavior of man, with all of its refinement and complexity, forms only a part of the behaviorist's total scheme of investigation.'

Behaviourism would have no truck with the inaccessible internal events of the mind. Indeed, many committed behaviourists would deny the validity of the concept of 'mind', saying that the mind doesn't exist. To start with, Watson was inclined to an epiphenomenalist view (that mental events are the by-products of physical processes but can't affect the body). Later, he took a physical-monist view, which he stated in no uncertain terms:

'[Consciousness] has never been seen, touched, smelled, tasted, or moved. It is a plain assumption, just as unprovable as the old concept of the soul.'

Instead, the behaviourist would approach human experience and nature purely through what can be observed and measured – behaviour.

John Broadus Watson photographed in 1929.

JOHN BROADUS WATSON (1878–1958)

Watson was born in South Carolina to a fiercely religious mother and an alcoholic father. His unusual middle name was in honour of a Baptist minister. His mother's religious fervour, with her corresponding condemnation of smoking, drinking and dancing, left him with an abiding hatred for religion. When Watson was 13 years old, his father left the family and went to live with two Cherokee women.

Watson was not a good student to start with. He was described as lazy and insubordinate, and he was twice arrested during his school years (once for fighting with African Americans, and once for shooting a gun in a public place). Even so, he used his mother's contacts to get a place at Furman University and graduated successfully.

After a year working as a school janitor, he went to university in Chicago to study philosophy under John Dewey (see page 64). He gained his PhD for a study of the learning process in white rats. In 1909 he became editor of the *Psychological Review*, succeeding James Baldwin, who was fired after being caught in a brothel. Watson used the position to publish his views on behaviourism. Ironically, Watson lost his own position at Johns Hopkins University in 1920 after he had an affair with his graduate student/research assistant Rosalie Rayner. Watson and his wife divorced, and he married Rayner, but their happiness was relatively short-lived, as she died aged 36.

After being forced to leave academia, Watson carved out a career in advertising. He began at the bottom, in a job he was offered by a contact of Titchener's, but was phenomenally successful, bringing his extensive knowledge of human behaviour and psychology to bear – the first time that psychology had been applied in advertising. Within two years, he was vice president of the agency J. Walter Thompson (now JWT). He continued to publish, though now in the popular press and in books for the lay reader, largely on childcare. He is particularly famous for the 'Little Albert' experiment (see page 120) and for his approach to parenting, which he felt should be a business-like arrangement, not sullied by affection between parent and child.

Watson used his knowledge of psychology in advertising campaigns for Maxwell House Coffee.

Behaviourism wasn't immediately popular. It represented a significant shift in psychological thought and method, and so took a while to catch on. But when it did, it came to dominate psychology for a large part of the 20th century. For around forty years it went unchallenged as the most important school. Some of the most famous and ground-breaking experiments in 20th-century psychology were behaviourist projects.

Watson began with an interest in Pavlov's findings in classical conditioning using dogs as experimental animals (see panel). Watson took instincts, reflexes and conditioning as his starting point and set out to explain all human behaviour in that model. Accordingly, he spent a lot of time working with young children, in whom it is easiest to see instincts clearly at work, unclouded by the fog of extensive experience and learning. He and other behaviourists – such as Edward Thorndike, Edward Tolman and B.F. Skinner – valued work with animals, too.

DRIBBLE AND DROOL

Classical conditioning was famously discovered by the Russian scientist Ivan Pavlov (1849–1936) working with dogs around 1903. Initially investigating the reflex that leads the dogs to salivate and produce stomach juices in response to the smell

or taste of meat, Pavlov moved on to train the dogs to expect food when they were exposed to a certain stimulus, such as the sound of a bell, metronome or whistle. Once the dogs associated the sound with the food, they would salivate on hearing it, even if the food was not present. He called this a conditioned reflex (now usually called a conditioned response). He carried out similar experiments with children, which would now be regarded as highly unethical.

Comparative psychology

The behaviourists were the first psychologists to make extensive use of studies using animals. With methods that depended on introspection, such as those of the structuralist and functionalist schools, animals clearly could not make suitable subjects. For the behaviourists, though, they were ideal. There was no possibility of the subjects modifying their behaviour to please or frustrate a researcher, no way the researcher could influence behaviour unfairly, and no temptation to look for mental events behind the manifest behaviour. Many of the behaviourists, Watson included, worked with white rats (a favourite laboratory animal because they are clever, small, easy to look after and reach maturity quite quickly). Edward Thorndike (see page 122) worked with cats; Edward Tolman worked with rats (see page 80); B.F. Skinner worked with rats and pigeons (see page 80).

'Let it be noted that rats live in cages; they do not go on binges the night before one has planned an experiment; they do not kill each other off in wars...they do not go in for either class conflicts or race conflicts; they avoid politics, economics and papers on psychology. They are marvellous, pure and delightful.'

Edward Tolman (1945)

Doing it on purpose

Watson didn't have it all his own way. William McDougall (1871–1938), a British-born psychologist who took up the chair of psychology at Harvard in 1920, focused his attention on purposive behaviour. It was easy for Watson, with his focus on reflexive behaviour, to ignore or deny the mind. But with behaviour that is initiated by the individual, and is not a response to an identifiable stimulus, it's harder to account for an action without looking for something resembling the mind. McDougall distinguished purposive behaviour as:

- goal oriented;
- not initiated by an environmental stimulus;
- variable – we will try different ways of reaching the goal;

- persistent – it will endure unless stopped by an environmental stimulus or until the goal is reached;
- improving – we get better at achieving our goals, through trial and error or practice.

In place of the external stimuli that prompt reflexive behaviour, McDougall cited instinctual motives as the drive behind purposive behaviour. In its simplest form, this could be the instinct to find food when hungry. An instinct produces changes in perception (noticing food when hungry), behaviour (doing things to get or find food), and emotion (feeling positive towards events related to getting food, such as a suggestion to go to a restaurant). Most of the time, though, instincts do not act alone, but in configurations. Two or more instincts associated with an idea form a sentiment. His list of instincts included escape, repulsion, mating, curiosity, food-seeking, assertion, laughter, parental protection and combat.

Watson rejected instincts as part of human psychology and believed that all learning could be accounted for by associations (see page 120), which lay at the heart of classical (Pavlovian) conditioning. This put him at odds with McDougall, whose model centred on instincts and who thought learning was based on reinforcement – behaviours found to be successful in meeting goals being repeated. The two had a famous debate in Washington DC in 1929, each putting his case forcefully. McDougall, who had pointed out that Watson's model could not account for the pleasure of listening to violin music, won by a narrow margin.

'I come into this hall and see a man on this platform scraping the guts of a cat with hairs from the tail of a horse; and, sitting silently in attitudes of rapt attention, are a thousand persons who presently break out into wild applause. How will the Behaviorists explain these strange incidents?...Common sense and psychology agree in accepting the explanation that the audience heard the music with keen pleasure...But the Behaviorist knows nothing of pleasure and pain, or admiration and gratitude. He has relegated all such "metaphysical entities" to the dust heap, and must seek some other explanation. Let us leave him seeking it. The search will keep him harmlessly occupied for some centuries to come.'

William McDougall (1929)

More behaviourism

Watson was a thorough positivist: he believed objective data to be the only valid and reliable goal of science. He also wanted psychology to be useful in producing predictions for behaviour and suggesting ways of controlling behaviour (his career in advertising showed that interest in action). The two aims were not entirely compatible as, without any explanation for the behaviours he observed, how was he to use them to make predictions? The only possibility for Watson was classical conditioning.

Another answer, for behaviourism in general, came from logical positivism. Under behaviourists such as the Americans Edward Tolman (1886–1959), Clark

Leonard Hull (1884–1952) and, finally, B.F. Skinner (1904–90), behaviourism was allowed to creep away from the atomistic, discrete, micro-behaviours of Watson's studies to encompass whole behaviours such as (in Tolman's words):

'a man driving home to dinner or a child hiding from a stranger.'

Cognition creeps back

Ultimately, Tolman accepted purpose and cognition, letting them back into the behaviourist camp, by rebadging them as 'intervening variables' that come between environmental events and behaviour. An event in the environment (independent variable) would cause some internal mental event (intervening variable) that then resulted in an observable behaviour (dependent variable). The internal events were allowed as they were thoroughly defined logically, tied to observable behaviour.

By involving purpose and cognition in his model, Tolman was moving away from the behaviourist model championed by Watson and towards the cognitive school that developed later in the 20th century. Unfortunately, his theory introduced such a degree of complexity with its numerous intervening variables that it was not possible for him to process all the information in an era before powerful computers. Tolman's influence endures in the popularity of cognitive behaviour therapy (CBT), which has developed at least in part from his model of purposive behaviour and mental constructs.

Drive reduction

Another development in behaviourism came from Clark Leonard Hull, who also took behaviourism in the cognitive direction. Hull believed that reinforcement was key to learning. In his model, a biological need created a drive and any behaviour that diminished the drive was reinforced. So, if you were too hot and felt a biological compulsion to become cooler, taking your jumper off would reduce the drive by

beginning the cooling process and so you would learn to take off your jumper when too hot. Repeated reinforcement leads to forming a habit. It resembles Tolman's model in having an intervening variable between stimulus and behaviour, but in this case the intervening variable is physiological (a biological drive) rather than mental.

Latent learning

Tolman did not believe a drive was always necessary to initiate learning. His behavioural studies with rats led him to the conclusion that we are learning all the time, but learning is latent until needed. In terms of his rats, they learned the maze, whether or not they needed to. If they were put in the maze when already sated, they noticed where food was located but did not go to it or eat it. If returned to the maze later on when they were hungry, they could go straight to the food as they had learned where it would be.

Tolman proposed that the rats built up a cognitive map of the world around them that developed through a pattern of hypothesis-building and mental trial and error. When a hypothesis was confirmed it became more firmly embedded, eventually becoming a belief. He emphasized learning of links between stimuli, so rather than an S-R (stimulus-response) theory his can be seen as a S1-S2 theory.

Back to behaviour

B.F. Skinner was the most famous of the behaviourists and one of the most important psychologists of the 20th century. He returned to Watson's position of refusing to pay any attention to mental events, even as some kind of intervening variable. He felt that nothing was lost by sticking with a functional analysis of the environment and behaviour, arguing that if there were any mental events, they weren't accessible so nothing is gained by thinking about them. He saw no place in science for the 'self' and whatever mental events it might have.

> 'A completely independent science of subjective experience would have no more bearing on a science of behaviour than a science of what people feel about fire would have on the science of combustion.'
>
> B.F. Skinner (1974)

Skinner, too, experimented with rats, using them to study learning in response to stimuli. He used a specially designed box that allowed him to try a variety of stimuli with rats and determine how they learned best. Skinner felt that behaviourism should have practical uses and benefits for society, and gave advice on education based on the evidence of his experiments with rats. Further, he promoted the use of behaviour modification as a form of therapy for people with unwanted behaviours such as addiction, phobias and social disorders. He believed that people had gained some form of reinforcement for these behaviours in the past, and that to modify their behaviour it was necessary to reinforce alternative types of behaviour.

Championing the human

The behaviourists had conducted a great deal of their work through experiments using animal subjects. It was a central tenet of behaviourism that animal learning and human learning were comparable as it was all down to biology. Because the behaviourists were not concerned with any mental events, and generally denied the existence of them, it was often easier, and just as valid, to experiment with animals as it was with people. That would not hold for the two schools of psychology that emerged in the second half of the 20th century. Both were exclusively concerned with aspects of human cognition and mental structures.

Psychologist Abraham Maslow, who championed a humanistic theory of self-actualization.

The first, humanistic psychology, set out to explore such topics as how we see and mould ourselves as human beings, how we find meaning in life, what drives us, and what it means to be human. It is concerned with motivation, personal growth, goals and the self. Clearly, cats, rats and pigeons in puzzle boxes are not going to be much help with this endeavour.

The humanistic approach to psychology originates with the work of Abraham Maslow (1908–70). Born in New York to a mother he hated, and the youngest of seven children, he didn't have an easy start in life. As a child he was classified as mentally unstable, and he suffered anti-Semitic bullying. He worked for a while with Alfred Adler (1870–1937), an early colleague of Freud's, and the experience persuaded him that he wanted to focus on the psychology of the healthy mind – a happier path than chasing psychological disturbance. Even so, he was not reacting entirely against Adler's approach, since Maslow – like Freud and Adler before him – focused on the experiences and personal accounts of individuals. He set out to discover the sources of personal strength and fulfilment, and examined the drives that motivate people in normal life. The most famous aspect of his work is his 'hierarchy of needs', still frequently cited in management psychology, and the concepts of 'self-actualization' (see page 157 [Chapter 6: *Becoming yourself*]) and 'peak experiences'.

Maslow and the co-founder of the humanistic school, fellow American Carl Rogers (1902–87), rejected an empirical scientific approach altogether. Instead, they used qualitative and subjective methods such as looking at biographical and autobiographical accounts, conducting open-ended questionnaires, unstructured interviews and observations, and case studies. Their aim was to find out from people who had made a success of life exactly how they had done it. Maslow and Rogers focused on individual experiences, finding richness in the subjectivity that would not have been possible with a more rigorously scientific approach. We will see more of their work in Chapter 6: *What Makes You 'You'?*.

Cognitive approaches

Cognitive psychology was the second 20th-century method that rejected animal experimentation. It's a broad category, as psychology by definition is concerned with cognition and mental acts, albeit that the foray into behaviourism neglected those aspects for a few decades. Modern cognitive psychology takes a range of approaches, including information-processing, cybernetics, linguistics and neurology in addition to mainstream psychological traditions. Accordingly, although a lot of cognitive psychology research is conducted through laboratory or field experiments with human subjects, some also makes extensive use of computer technologies.

Problems in cognitive experimentation

Experiments with human subjects, unless they are looking entirely at behaviour with no cognitive background, invariably have an element of chaos and subjectivity. It has been common in the past to tell subjects that they are being tested or observed in one way when the researcher is actually interested in a different aspect. This puts subjects off their guard. They might pay extra attention to the aspect they believe is being observed, thereby changing that behaviour, but they will act more naturally in other regards – including, the researchers hope, the aspect that is the subject of their investigation.

For example, a group of volunteers are invited to sit in a room and answer a written intelligence test. While they're doing that, someone steals a wallet from the jacket of a member of the group. The volunteers think they are there solely to do the test. In fact, they are being studied to see how they react to the apparent theft.

Cognitive psychology is a very varied field best grasped through the various studies we will see later.

Social psychology

Social psychology, another 20th-century development, looks at how people behave in groups (and therefore in relation to others). It grew in influence after the Second World War when psychologists became interested in the ways some people behave towards those with greater or lesser power. Some of the most famous studies in psychology belong to this school, including Stanley Milgram's study of obedience (see page 171 [Chapter 7: *Follow the crowd*]) and Phil Zimbardo's study of how prisoners and prison guards behave if given free rein (see page 166–167 [Chapter 7: *Are we good or bad?*]).

Many social psychology experiments are field experiments, but not all situations can be found or staged in the real world. Zimbardo's experiment, for example,

could not have been staged by observing a real prison as the behaviour of guards is constrained by regulations. Clearly an experiment in a laboratory lacks certain types of authenticity, and there are always questions to ponder about how far the results can be extended to normal situations outside the laboratory. On the other hand, a field study does not allow the researcher full control of the variables.

An example makes this clearer. In 1968, Irving and Jane Piliavin set out to investigate bystander behaviour in an emergency. The researchers hired actors to board a crowded train on the New York subway and fake a collapse. The researchers were present as observers and studied the responses of passengers. They repeated the experiment with different 'victims' and approaches. Three of the 'victims' were white and one was black but all dressed alike. Each one either pretended to be drunk, or remained sober but carried a walking stick (implying a disability). These were the variables the researchers could control. They had no control over possible 'confounding variables', such as how many people would be present in the train compartment at the time, and how representative they were of society in general.

The researchers were interested in the speed with which help was offered, the gender and racial profile of the people helping, and how often help was offered. They found that more men than women helped, and that the drunk victims were helped less often than the stick-carrying victims (nearly half compared to 95 per cent). The researchers concluded that in situations like this people subconsciously carry out a cost/reward assessment, balancing the cost to themselves of helping (perhaps disgust, embarrassment, risk of assault or getting covered in vomit) against the rewards they can anticipate (being praised, not having to worry later). They found, counter to other studies, that the number of people in the carriage did not affect people's readiness to help. Generally, the 'bystander effect' means people are less likely to help if there are other people present, as responsibility is dissipated and it's easier to think 'it's not my job' (see page 171 [Chapter 7: *Follow the crowd*]).

Pick and mix

Since the late 20th century, psychology has no longer been dominated by any one

particular school. It is rather an eclectic mix of methods that co-exist amicably. As such, it employs a number of experimental methods that have been used in the past, but also some new ones that take advantage of technologies not previously available.

Areas of brain function, for instance, can be investigated using functional MRI (fMRI) scanners to show which parts of the brain are working when a particular stimulus is applied or activity carried out. Brain scans also compare the structures of different brains. There are, for instance, distinctive characteristics in the brains of psychopaths when compared with the brains of non-psychopaths (see page 190) or in the brains of taxi drivers with highly developed

Are we less likely to help someone if other people are present?

ROUTE MASTERS

In 2000, Eleanor Maguire at University College, London, used magnetic resonance imaging (MRI) to study the brains of London taxi drivers. She compared scans of their brains with those of a control group of men of similar age and profile. She noticed that the taxi drivers had significantly larger posterior hippocampi than the control group. This area of the brain is important in navigation and spatial awareness. To qualify as London cabbies, drivers must spend up to four years learning routes through the 25,000 streets of London (a process known as acquiring 'The Knowledge'), so their hippocampi get plenty of exercise. She concluded that this part of the brain can adapt with use, expanding like an exercised muscle. The taxi drivers also had a smaller anterior hippocampus than the control group, suggesting that this had shrunk to make room for the expansion. She found that the longer the men had worked as taxi drivers, the more marked the difference between their brains and those of the control group. In a follow-up study, she examined retired taxi drivers, and found that the size shrunk again when the posterior hippocampus was no longer being used extensively. While the taxi drivers played a computer simulation of driving, she examined their brains in action using an fMRI scanner and found the hippocampus was active while the drivers were thinking about the route. As important as showing the area of the brain that is used in navigation was her finding that the brain can adapt and grow, even in a fully grown adult.

navigational knowledge compared with a control group (see panel).

Further, psychology has become increasingly interdisciplinary. More and more studies are in applications of psychology, including therapy, education, management, marketing, sociology, computing, social engineering and political science. It's become hard to say where psychology begins and ends.

CHAPTER 4

How do we
KNOW:
is knowledge innate or acquired?

*'It is the soul that sees and hears; not [the eyes and ears],
which are but windows to the soul; by means of which the
soul can perceive nothing, unless she is on the spot and
exerts herself.'*

Roman philosopher Cicero (106–43 BC), *The Tusculan
Príbor Disputations* (c.45 BC)

**One of the principal functions of the brain is
to know things. How we obtain knowledge
has taxed philosophers and psychologists for
millennia. There are several models of the
brain at birth (see Chapter 5: *Making the Mind*)
but whatever the starting position,
we need to populate the brain with new
knowledge. What is going on in the brain
when we learn? How do we actually 'know'
things and store that knowledge? How do we
choose what to remember? How do we recall
it later? And why do we forget some of it, yet
seem incapable of forgetting other, traumatic,
things that we would rather forget?**

Facing page: *Are we born knowing, or do we acquire
knowledge through perception and experience?*

Ways of knowing

Demonstrative and empirical knowledge

The English philosopher David Hume (1711–76) believed there to be only two valid types of knowledge, 'demonstrative' and 'empirical' knowledge. Demonstrative knowledge is abstract. It is produced by imagination and reason, and works by putting together ideas that don't necessarily have any correlation to the real world. Mathematical and other theoretical knowledge falls into this category. Empirical knowledge is based on experience and is the more reliable and useful. Everything else he considered to be 'sophistry and illusion', including all religion and metaphysics.

Following Hume's model, building knowledge can happen in one of two ways: it can involve the outside world, or it can be entirely internal. If you see a dog walking down the street, the new knowledge – that there is a dog walking down the street – involves processing information about the world from your senses. It is empirical. However, if you are just thinking about whether you like dogs, you are working with ideas you have formed already – it is a process that is wholly internal to the mind. It is demonstrative. Philosophers have held different views about the relative reliability of different sources of knowledge.

Rationalism versus empiricism

Demonstrative and empirical knowledge relates to broadly different schools of thought that can be traced back to ancient Greece: 'empiricism' and 'rationalism'. Empiricism prioritizes evidence from the external world in constructing knowledge. Aristotle championed this view, considering only the information that we can test with our own senses to be a solid basis for reasoning and knowledge. The opposite – rationalist – view, looks to reason to provide knowledge. Plato was a rationalist, arguing that our senses can only perceive reality imperfectly and so sense impressions are not a reliable basis for knowledge. Instead reason, as the highest and distinguishing faculty of humankind, was the only way to arrive at secure knowledge.

In the late 16th and early 17th centuries, empiricism and rationalism each had a great spokesman who set the terms for a

Philosopher David Hume.

debate that would develop over the coming centuries. In the empiricist corner was the English philosopher and scientist Francis Bacon (1561–1626), who distrusted reason and believed that the only reliable knowledge was based on observation of the real world. As we can only perceive the real world through our senses, sensory perceptions are then key to understanding. People are, in his view, prone to adhere to ideas and biases they already have and allow these to colour their perceptions when thinking theoretically. They are also prone to arguing about the meaning of words rather than the actual nature of phenomena. His attitude, that all valid knowledge can be verified by empirical observation, is one that would later be called 'positivism'.

On the other hand, the French philosopher René Descartes (1596–1650) championed reason. Unable to trust his perception of the outside world, he decided that if he started with his cognition he could incrementally build a body of reliable knowledge without depending on his senses, so he was a 'rationalist'. Descartes' influence was so great that most European philosophers over the following century set out their stalls answering, supporting or challenging aspects of Cartesian philosophy.

Perception is real, but what about the perceived?

Hume, who was one of the most important British empiricists, claimed that all we have to go on in creating knowledge is our perceptions, and we can have no confidence in the existence of anything other than the fact that we have sensory experiences. The question of whether what we perceive actually relates to reality is unanswerable. He was not the only one to think this; the 5th-century Sophists had declared that there is no such thing as certain knowledge. The German psychologist Franz Brentano (1838–1917) claimed that while we can be absolutely certain of our perceptions – we can be sure we hear a tone or see a ball – we can't be at all sure that the perception relates to anything in the external world. The fact of hearing or seeing he called internal perception; sensory perception – perceptions that appear to be of the external world – he considered to be capable only of giving us theories about what is 'out there' – not facts.

Common sense

Someone had to say it, and Hume's contemporary Thomas Reid did. Whether or not Hume rationally believed in the evidence of his senses, Reid said common sense dictates that we all rely on our senses in order to get through life; for anyone, even Hume, to believe otherwise

complex train of thought were necessary to understand our perceptions.

Immanuel Kant (1724–1804), one of the most influential and important of all philosophers, agreed with Hume on the unreliability of the senses. He referred to the objects that constitute external reality, the 'things-in-themselves' that are 'out there', as noumena. He agreed that we can know nothing about them with any certainty as they are only mediated through our senses. What we can know about are phenomena

would lead to them being 'clapped into a madhouse'. Indeed, Reid didn't believe that we need reason at all in order to interpret the evidence of our senses – we just perceive things directly, with no processing of sensations. As evidence, he pointed out that children – and indeed many adults – have no reasoning powers and so would gain no benefit from their senses and be unable to live effectively if a

In the Matrix *films, the world that the characters live in is an illusion created by a computer. Can we be certain of our own perceptions?*

– the appearances of noumena as they have been modified by sensory perception and categories of thought. The categories of thought were the significant point of difference with Hume; there is more about them in Chapter 5: *Making the Mind.*

Sensation and perception

However reliable or unreliable our senses may be as mediators of the outside world (if there is one), they are, as Reid said, all we have to go on. Our psychological interaction with the outside world, and the world of our own physical body, takes place through the processes of sensation and perception. The two are intimately linked but discrete. Sensation is the process of sensing through the physical senses of vision, hearing, touch, and taste and other sensory mechanisms such as feeling pain or heat. Perception is the act of making meaning from that, of understanding the sensory information. The two are often run together in the composite 'sense perception' when psychologists are not distinguishing between the two.

Touch is one way we make sense of the world around us.

Back to the ghost and the machine

In order for sensation to lead to perception, we must suppose either that the body and mind communicate or that they are one and the same thing. Suppose you cut your finger. There are different levels of response:

- Your finger bleeds: this is a mechanical response, following the laws of matter and fluid dynamics. It's the same as if you cut a pipe through which water was pumped.
- You feel pain: this is a shared physical and mental event and this is where the body and mind need to work together. The pain begins as the stimulation of a nerve, a sensation. In the brain, the sensation is interpreted (perceived) as pain.
- You might also feel anger, shock, or some other emotion related to having been hurt: this occurs inside the mind through processes of association. It does not come from the nerves stimulated by the cut.

The Greek physician Alcmaeon of Croton (5th century BC) might have been the first person to dissect the human body. By tracing the optic nerve from the eye to the brain, either in humans or animals, he discovered the connection between the senses and the brain. He tested the function of the optic nerve by severing it in animals and testing the outcome. He concluded that all perception, thought, memory and understanding were carried out by the brain, even though the source information came from the sensory organs. We agree with Alcmaeon now,

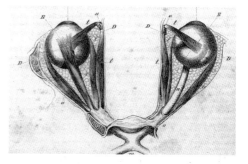

A 19th-century sketch of the optic nerve.

91

but plenty of thinkers between his time and ours have seen the process rather differently.

The ancient Greek philosopher Epicurus (341–270BC), who was a physical monist, suggested that the psyche is made of very fine matter that is distributed throughout the physical body, so body and mind are an aggregate. Acts of sensation and perception are possible because the mind is integrated into the body parts, so readily works in sympathy with them.

The Roman philosopher Lucretius (99–55BC) believed the soul to be separate and divided it into a thinking part (*animus*) and a sensing part (*anima*). The thinking part, he said, is located in the chest, but the sensing part is distributed throughout the body. The *animus* can cut itself off from the body, but the *anima* can't. In cases of strong emotion, both are inextricably involved.

For the Stoics, the sympathy between body and psyche was sufficient to prove that the psyche is one and the same thing as the body:

'No incorporeal interacts with a body, and no body with an incorporeal, but one body interacts with another body. Now the soul interacts with the body when it is sick and being cut, and the body with the soul; thus when the soul feels shame and fear the body turns red and pale respectively. Therefore, the soul is a body.'
Christian philosopher Nemesius (c.AD390)

On human understanding

In 1689, the English physician and philosopher John Locke (1632–1704) published the book that kick-started modern

ALL DOWN TO US – AND ATOMS

The Greek scientist-philosopher Democritus (c.460–370BC) was the first to propose an entirely physical means for perception (and, indeed, everything else). With no recourse to gods, he described impressions in terms of the five physical senses receiving 'atoms' emanating from the physical universe and relaying them to the brain. Here, the mobile 'fire atoms' of the brain make copies of the objects. The copies may not be accurate, so there can be a mismatch between what we perceive and what exists.

Democritus is often regarded as the father of modern science.

empiricism and might be considered the first full-length text to tackle aspects of psychology. *An Essay Concerning Human Understanding* sets out to explain how the mind works – an ambitious undertaking. It had huge influence, not least on Bishop George Berkeley and David Hume.

Locke was the first to propose in detail a model of how we construct knowledge. He considered the mind has only two types of material to work with, and so all knowledge comes either directly from sensations or from reflection. Sense perceptions are the information received through our sensory organs, such as eyes and ears; reflection he explained as 'the perception of the operations of our own mind within us, as it is employed about the ideas it has got'. As reflection works on digested earlier perceptions, which in turn also came from sensations, it all comes down to sensations in the end. The interface between the world and the mind is, then, perception. We forge knowledge by making associations between ideas – and ideas themselves are formed from perceptions and the sensations they leave behind in the mind. So, sorting out how perceptions are produced is crucial to understanding how we acquire knowledge. (Note that there are two types of 'sensation'

Enlightenment philosopher John Locke.

here – one is the stimulation of nerves in a sensory organ, and the other is an echo of perception left in the mind and which can be revived for a later perception-by-reflection.)

Perception and apperception

Gottfried Leibniz (he of the monads) was interested in how each perception is made up of infinitely tiny perceptions, which he called 'petites perceptions'. He was famous also for developing calculus independently of Isaac Newton. His view of perception accords well with his interest in calculus, which also deals with micro-portions that tend towards the infinitely small yet never quite approach zero.

Leibniz gave as an example of a 'petite perception' the experience of listening to the sound of crashing waves. It is, he points out, made up of perceptions of lots of small movements of water, some so small that we would not be consciously aware of them if they occurred alone. Yet clearly we are aware of them, as they combine to make us consciously aware of the sound of the sea, and a sensation can't be made up from a lot of nothings. For him, the point at which there is sufficient mass of micro-perceptions to be noticeable is

called 'apperception' – so apperception is the point of awareness. There is also a threshold, or 'limen', below which the perceptions we have remain unconscious. He was possibly the first philosopher to give a clear proposal of an unconscious mind. Leibniz's limen was explored experimentally in the psychophysics experiments of the 19th century, measured as the 'just noticeable difference' by Weber and Fechner (see page 48 [Chapter 2: *Psychophysics*]).

Creating the world by perceiving it

Bishop George Berkeley (1685–1753) made the mind do even more work with sense-perceptions. Alarmed at the way materialism was eroding the domain of God, he threw out materialist arguments wholesale, along with matter, and adopted an idealist position (the only reality is ideas). Berkeley contended that all we have are our sense perceptions and that they are what create the world for us:

'All those bodies which compose the mighty frame of the world, have not any subsistence without a mind; that their being is to be perceived or known; that consequently so long as they are not actually perceived by me, or do not exist in my mind, or that of any other created spirit, they must either have no existence at all, or else subsist in the mind of some Eternal Spirit.'

His conclusion – that things don't exist if they are not being perceived – dumps on the mind all the responsibility for keeping the physical universe in existence. It's asking a lot. To get around the obvious problem that, for instance, the carrots you put in the fridge are there when you look later but apparently didn't exist when you shut the fridge door, Berkeley enlists the help of the divine.

When no 'created spirit' is keeping an eye on the material world, God takes over and keeps it going: 'When I shut my eyes, the things I saw may still exist; but it must be in another mind.'

Although it all sounds rather bizarre and far-fetched, Berkeley's account of perception was and is important because it shows how complex ideas are put together from multiple sense-perceptions. We might dispute whether there really is no such thing as a tree, but when he extends the same principle to abstracts that we perceive, he has a good point. We put together the idea of a tree from our perception of its size, shape, smell, the feel of the bark, the rustling of the leaves. Similarly we put together the idea of someone's anger or shame from how they look, move, speak and act. The mind has a huge amount to do to 'make' the world, even if it isn't also maintaining its physical existence.

Experimental work on perception

The early experimental work of the 19th century focused on perception and sensation. First Weber and Fechner, and then Wundt, and later the structuralist and functionalist psychologists, all used empirical physical methods to study the thresholds of perception and then the possible elements of perception. In Edward Titchener's studies, for example, introspective analysis might reveal that a subject perceived the distinctive taste and smell of a fruit, and its colour, shape, solidity, texture, and weight. Titchener would have classed these as separated sensory experiences that the mind puts together to experience an apple or an orange. Müller's work on the nerves demonstrated that the eyes sensed the colour and the nose the smell of the fruit (see page 45 [Chapter 2: *Putting together the pieces*]). The brain then translates the

information from the eyes into a visual image of, say, orange and round.

Starting to know

There is a big difference between perceiving a pattern of light or sounds and understanding or interpreting it. Information that is sent from the sensory organs to the brain is processed in order to be perceived, but then the brain needs to do more work with it to know what it means, to store it for later, or to act on it. Once the brain has received information from the senses observing an apple or an orange, it does a lot of work to construct and recognize the fruit.

Association

Aristotle believed the mind – or our 'common sense' – makes links between sensations and events, largely based on their appearing close to one another in time or space, or occurring together frequently. The mind also associates things that are similar, and sometimes even things that contrast with one another (such as hot and cold, or sweet and sour). These associations are the basis of knowledge. He believed that common sense is responsible for bringing together all aspects or 'elements' of something to create the idea of it. So it might bring together colour, smell, shape, texture and taste to produce the idea of an orange, for instance. This association of ideas was accepted for two millennia without much further investigation until David Hume took it up again in the 18th century.

Associationism flourishes

The English physician and philosopher David Hartley (1705–57) asserted that if we consistently experience several events or sensations together, our minds store them as a package. Encountering just one of the set then recalls all the others, too. For Hartley, the key aspect of association was contiguity – that ideas or impressions that were always encountered together 'clumped' in that way. Hartley made the first attempt to give a physical account of how sense impressions became ideas in the mind. He proposed that sense perceptions produce vibrations in the nerves that travel to the brain and cause corresponding vibrations there. These brain vibrations produce sensations. When the sensation

LAWS OF ASSOCIATION

There are generally considered to be three or four ways in which the mind uses association to build ideas from 'elements'. (When three are listed, it's usually the law of similarity that is missing; contiguity and frequency are the most important.)

1. The law of contiguity: things that occur close together in space or time are linked by the mind. If you think of a fork, you might also think of a knife to go with it.

2. The law of frequency: if two things or events are linked, the association between them will be stronger the more frequently you come across them together. If your grandma always gave you home-baked cakes, you are likely to think of her in association with home-baked cakes.

3. The law of similarity: the mind associates similar things. If you find one sock on the floor, you will think about the other, matching sock and wonder where it might be.

4. The law of contrast: sometimes, seeing or thinking something will trigger thoughts of its opposite. If you think about your best friend at school, you might also recall the class bully you hated.

has passed, slight echoes or remnants of the vibrations exist, called (rather prettily) 'vibratiuncles'. These correspond to ideas, and are the same as the original sensations but weaker. Complex ideas are constructed from associations between simple ideas, and complex ideas can themselves coalesce into even more complex ('decomplex') ideas. Hartley's account of how associations form and how mental events correlate to biology remained authoritative for eighty years.

The Scottish philosopher James Mill (1773–1836) took Hartley's ideas of association further and made it the foundation of all that the mind can do. For him, all ideas comprised several originally separate simple ideas that were always thought of together, and so our comprehension of physical objects is really just a collection of perceptions that can't be separated:

'It is to the great law of association, that we trace the formation of ideas of what we call external objects; that is, the idea of a certain number of sensations, received together so frequently that they coalesce as it were, and are spoken of under the idea of unity. Hence, what we call the idea of a tree, the idea of a stone, the idea of a horse, the idea of a man.'

'And suddenly the memory returns. The taste was that of the little crumb of madeleine which on Sunday mornings at Combray...my aunt Léonie used to give me, dipping it first in her own cup of real or of lime-flower tea...

And once I had recognized the taste of the crumb of madeleine soaked in her decoction of lime-flowers...immediately the old grey house upon the street, where her room was, rose up like the scenery of a theatre to attach itself to the little pavilion, opening on to the garden, which had been built out behind it for my parents (the isolated panel which until that moment had been all that I could see); and with the house the town, from morning to night and in all weathers, the Square where I was sent before luncheon, the streets along

which I used to run errands, the country roads we took when it was fine...in that moment all the flowers in our garden and in M. Swann's park, and the water-lilies on the Vivonne and the good folk of the village and their little dwellings and the parish church and the whole of Combray and of its surroundings, taking their proper shapes and growing solid, sprang into being, town and gardens alike, all from my cup of tea.'
Marcel Proust (1871–1922),
Remembrance of Things Past (1913–27)

Simple ideas associate to make complex ideas, and complex ideas can be combined to make more complex (duplex) ideas, which in turn can be combined...and so on. But the reducibility of everything to basic ideas that were perceptions is the key point. Associations are stronger or weaker according to how vivid they are and how frequently the ideas are encountered together.

Psychology accomplished

Mill's account of association was the fullest expression of it. He explained how the mind automatically works with its basic elements – sensations – following the laws of association to produce all the mental apparatus we enjoy as humans. He felt he had successfully constructed a 'physics of the mind' comparable with Newtonian physics and its explanation of the

John Stuart Mill.

universe in terms of its elemental matter irrevocably following immutable physical laws. There were two rather unappealing aspects of Mill's model, though. The first is that the mind does nothing creative; it is, as Descartes and Hume wanted it to be, working like a machine and just following a set of rules. The second is that mental events become entirely predictable, just like physical events. There is no space for individuality, creativity, the spark of genius or free will.

Mill's son, John Stuart Mill (1806–73) took on board his father's thinking, with only slight variation. He argued that the science of human nature (psychology) was a precise science and would one day be fully understood so that we would be able to predict behaviour and thoughts. At present (he meant in the 19th century, but it's still true) the laws governing it are not properly known. But not knowing these laws doesn't mean they don't exist, and when they are discovered, the mystery of thought will be unravelled. He believed that once these primary laws were known, it would then be possible to explore and explain how individual personalities develop and predict behaviour in specific circumstances.

Rationalists put the mind to work

Let's return to the apple or orange for a moment. It's all very well to say that the senses deliver information to the brain and the components are put together to make the perception of an object, but what exactly are the components? We see the fruit is, say, orange and spherical. Orange is fair enough – it's a colour that doesn't really need processing. But spherical? That requires us to understand extension in space and to understand that although the fruit looks like a circle it is actually a sphere.

Immanuel Kant invoked innate categories of thought to make meaning from our sense perceptions (see page 109 [Chapter 5: *The organizing mind*]). According to Kant, there is nothing in sense perceptions to tell us that something is far away or nearby because the sense perception itself happens in our own body. It is only by applying thought categories that we manage to make these interpretations. Taking issue with Hume's contention that causation is not real, Kant argued that while we can't actually prove that an effect follows a particular cause, it

BOOKS FOR BURNING

The French philosopher Claude Helvetius (1715–71) was a significant influence on James Mill and the way he brought up his son, John Stuart. A wealthy tax collector married to a

countess, Helvetius followed the line of argument that everything in the mind is ultimately the result of experience to its logical conclusion: that if we control the experiences someone has, we can control how their mind will develop. This has obvious implications for education – if we can give people a perfect education, we can create perfect people. (It has more sinister implications, too.) Helvetius' first book, *Essays on the Mind* (1758) so angered the academics of the Sorbonne in Paris that it was burned.

The late 18th and early 19th centuries saw an increased interest in education. As a young boy John Stuart Mill received a rigorous education from his father at home.

FACULTY PSYCHOLOGY

Thomas Reid – who said Hume would be clapped in a madhouse if he didn't rely on his senses in day-to-day life – was an early proponent of 'faculty psychology'. This rests on the claim that the mind has many aspects or functions, called faculties, that interact. Reid identified 43 faculties, including reason, consciousness, compassion, memory, judgment, and morality. Kant was also a faculty psychologist, with his categories of thought.

seems to us that causation is real; thought categories organize experience in such a way that we see one thing causing another.

Helmholtz used 'unconscious inference' to explain how the mind made sense of perceptions. He said that we use our body of past experiences to understand what we see – so once we have seen a sufficient number of different chairs, we will be able to recognize a new one when we see it.

Our experience of viewing perspective in a three-dimensional world enables us to perceive that an orange is a sphere and not a disc. He experimented with distorting glasses and found that his subjects soon adjusted to them. Helmholtz's conclusion, that past experience builds sensations into perceptions, was an empiricist one. It differed from Kant's view – that categories of thought were innate and began to

operate on sensations straight from birth. Helmholtz believed the mind must first learn how to perceive. Modern rationalist psychologists favour a Kantian view of structures in the brain that pattern our thinking. Empiricists favour a view, like that of Helmholtz, that relies on sensory experience, learning and passive laws of association. They would say that through experience, we learn that an object that looks round is sometimes a sphere and sometimes a disc. With an unfamiliar object we can determine which it is from subtle effects of light and shade that we don't even notice we are seeing, but with a familiar object we draw on past experience to tell us that an orange is spherical but a pancake is a flat circle.

Perceiving and acting

The way we act is governed by how we perceive the world (that is, how our brains model it) rather than how it actually is. The Gestalt psychologist Kurt Koffka (1886–1941) distinguished between the geographical environment – the physical world around us – and the behavioural environment, which is our subjective interpretation of it. He told an old German story to illustrate this point: A man rides across what he believes to be a snowy plain. When he speaks to someone at the end of his journey, he learns that he has actually just ridden across a frozen lake that could have given way at any moment. When he realizes the danger he was in, the poor man falls down dead from shock.

The behaviour of the old man accords not with the environment as it really is but as he believed it to be. Had he known the true nature of the surface he was riding on he would not have taken that route. His subsequent behaviour, in falling down dead, puts his perception of danger into action – he does what he would have expected to do if he had known the true nature of his actions. Perception is all.

Snowy plain or frozen lake? And what difference does it make?

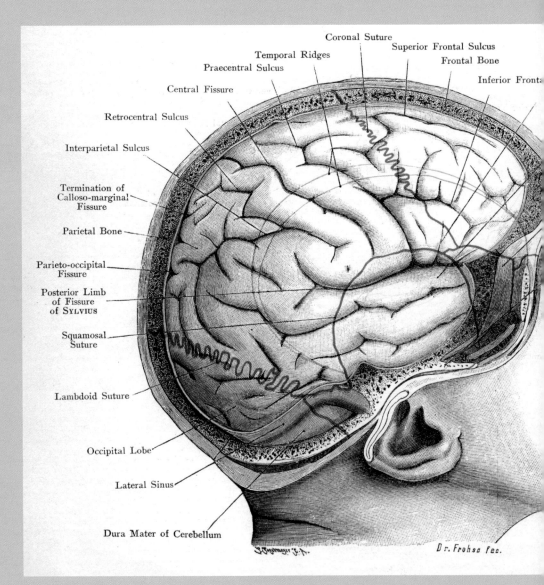

Coronal Suture

Temporal Ridges

Superior Frontal Sulcus

Praecentral Sulcus

Frontal Bone

Central Fissure

Inferior Fronta

Retrocentral Sulcus

Interparietal Sulcus

Termination of
Calloso-marginal
Fissure

Parietal Bone

Parieto-occipital
Fissure

Posterior Limb
of Fissure
of SYLVIUS

Squamosal
Suture

Lambdoid Suture

Occipital Lobe

Lateral Sinus

Dura Mater of Cerebellum

Dr. Frohse fec.

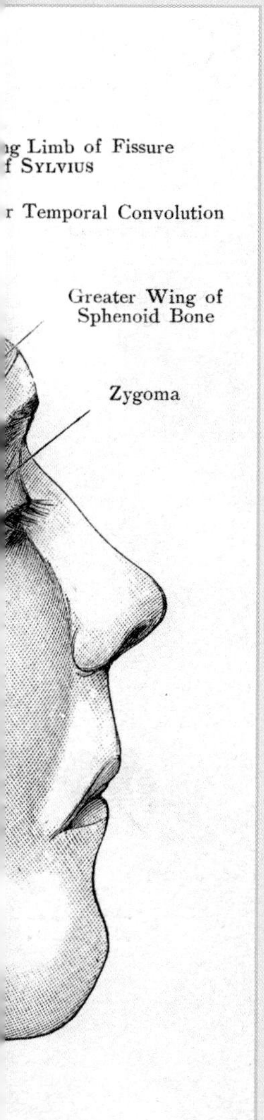

CHAPTER 5

Making the **MIND:**
the building blocks of the psyche

'Let us then suppose the mind to be, as we say, white paper, void of all characters, without any ideas: – How comes it to be furnished? Whence comes it by that vast store which the busy and boundless fancy of man has painted on it with an almost endless variety? To this I answer, in one word, from EXPERIENCE.'

John Locke, *An Essay Concerning Human Understanding* (1690)

If knowledge is built by processing sensory perceptions, or from further reflection on knowledge already acquired, what is the mind like to start with? Is it like a vast box into which perceptions are chucked willy-nilly? That would not make it very easy to recall knowledge when we need it. If not that way, how might the mind organize material and construct links between it? Is the mind involved at all, or is it all down to the way the brain is organized?

ng Limb of Fissure
f SYLVIUS

r Temporal Convolution

Greater Wing of
Sphenoid Bone

Zygoma

Facing page: *We can map the brain, but is the mind the same thing?*

What do babies know?

We all begin life as babies. What does the baby know, and how? There are two broad possibilities: that the infant's mind is a blank slate waiting for knowledge to be inscribed upon it, or that we are all born with some innate knowledge. A more refined position, part way between the two, proposes that the mind is born with certain structures that make it possible to organize knowledge in certain ways as it is acquired. The process of learning populates these structures with knowledge. The two extreme positions can be traced back to antiquity, while the midway position – the idea of the mind as 'organizer' – is more recent.

Born knowing

Psamtik I and others that conducted the 'forbidden experiments' (see page 37 [Chapter 2: *Child-as-guinea-pig*]) were not alone in believing that all humans are born with some innate knowledge. Plato believed that our souls have absolute knowledge when in their pure state, but when it enters a body the soul's access to that knowledge is cut off. He considered learning to be a process of uncovering innate knowledge rather than of discovery. This view can be called 'nativistic' in that it assumes there to be forms of knowledge that are native to the human state.

Much later, Descartes also proposed that some types of knowledge are innate. The most important of these, he claimed, was knowledge of God, which he considered to be common to all people. (He lived in

How much does a newborn baby know? Is knowledge innate or acquired?

16th-century France; to deny the existence of God was to risk being burnt as a heretic.) Other philosophers have suggested that some types of moral knowledge are innate.

Nativism is not restricted to knowledge. It can encompass any kind of inherited natural tendency or trait. The view that humans are innately savage and only kept in check by society, as Thomas Hobbes believed, is nativistic in that it relies on traits already present in the newborn individual. So is the opposite view, held by the French writer and philosopher Jean-Jacques Rousseau (1712–78), that humans are innately noble but corrupted by society. We will look at Rousseau's view later (see page 127).

Knowledge revealed

Plato supposed that the soul has perfect knowledge of all things and if it is not trapped inside the body it can see clearly. Once in the body, though, it loses instant access to knowledge and 'instead of investigating reality by itself, it is compelled to peer through the bars of its prison'. Knowledge is then revealed through the process of learning. He gave a proof of this concept in the form of an account of Socrates questioning a slave about geometry. At first, the slave seems to know nothing of geometry but as Socrates quizzes him, he slowly reveals an understanding. To Plato, this was clear proof that the slave had the knowledge innately but could not at first access it. In fact, it is far more likely that the slave was able to work out the answer through Socrates' careful prompting.

Gottfried Leibniz expressed a similar idea in the 18th century. His view that the whole universe is populated by points of consciousness called monads gave rise to his idea that the super-strength monads of the human mind had ideas that existed as potentialities until experience or sensory perception activated or actualized them. Just as a dark room might contain several objects that can't be seen until a light is turned on, so for Leibniz the mind contains innate ideas that may be uncovered later on.

Knowledge from the past

The French naturalist Jean-Baptiste Lamarck (1744–1829) proposed the theory that evolution occurred through the inheritance of acquired characteristics. Lamarck suggested that, during the course of its life, an organism adapts its physical form and behaviour to suit its environment. (The example often given is of the giraffe stretching up to reach the most succulent leaves and extending its neck in the process.) If the organism reproduces, its offspring inherit these acquired characteristics. Through this process, iterated over hundreds or thousands of generations, species change. The theory enjoyed some popular support before being eclipsed by Charles Darwin's theory of evolution by natural selection.

Lamarck's theory appealed to Herbert Spencer (1820–1903), a writer with an interest in psychology. He took Lamarck's view of physical evolution and applied it to the mind. The result was a theory that the mind has been slowly perfecting itself over time. The behaviours and beliefs that work well are reinforced, and those that are not beneficial are avoided in future. These lessons are passed on through

The flood (above) and the apocalypse (below) are examples of universal archetypes.

generations. During the course of one lifetime, reinforced behaviours become habits. Habits that have been developed by the parents are passed on to the offspring, and in those individuals appear as instincts since they are ingrained from birth.

The Swiss psychologist Carl Jung (1875–1961) worked with a similar concept to come up with his ideas about archetypes and the collective unconscious that recalls Spencer's theory about human behaviour accreting over the generations. The collective unconscious, according to Jung, is a bank of accumulated psychic structures built up over human evolution and evident most clearly in 'archetypes' that are found in different cultures throughout the world and which he claimed represent:

'[the] whole spiritual heritage of mankind's evolution, born anew in the brain structure of every individual.'

Jung had an interest in spirituality and at times his explanation of the collective unconscious seems to suggest that individuals can tap into some form of universal spirit, recalling the panpsychic views of Spinoza and Fechner. Elsewhere he describes it as simply a universal structure of the mind that predisposes all people to see and understand certain things in certain ways, just as we all share the same structure of the arm or leg.

Archetypes are psychic patterns that are equivalent to instincts. They can only be uncovered by comparing the myths, imagery and other cultural artefacts of different societies and discovering recurrent patterns in these conscious manifestations of the collective unconscious. Examples of archetypal images include figures such as the mother, the hero, the wise old woman or the trickster, and near-universal myths such as the flood and the apocalypse. They are also evident (actualized) in human institutions and celebrations such as marriage or coming-of-age rituals that mark archetypal stages of life.

These theories, from Plato and Psamtik to Jung, suggest innate knowledge – that the infant is born with some knowledge or types of knowledge in place, though perhaps waiting to be uncovered by reason or learning. In Jung's case, we are not aware of the knowledge of archetypes but it is made manifest in the social structures and art (and dreams) we produce. That is perhaps a position somewhere between innate knowledge and inherited mental structures, which we will look at soon (see pages 108–109).

A wedding is an archetype evident in everyday life.

The blank slate

The opposite view to that of the mind populated with innate knowledge is that the mind is an empty page on which experience and perception will leave their marks. Aristotle was the first to propose that the infant mind is empty. Around 1,300 years later, the Persian scholar Ibn Sina coined the phrase *tabula rasa* or 'blank slate' for the new, untutored mind: 'Human intellect at birth is like a *tabula rasa*, a pure potentiality that is actualized through education and comes to know.'

The Andalusian polymath Ibn Tufail (c.1105–85) wrote an early philosophical novel in which he described a young boy, Hayy, brought

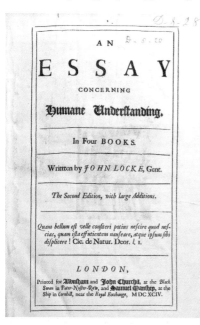

The title page from Locke's An Essay Concerning Human Understanding *(1690).*

Feral children provide psychologists with a rare but valuable chance to consider the role of nurture in knowledge acquisition.

up by a gazelle on a desert island. The feral child develops into a fully functioning adult, demonstrating the *tabula rasa* theory of learning. Further, Hayy manages to deduce ultimate truth through reason alone. The novel was translated into Latin in 1671, as *Theologus Autodidactus*, and into English in 1708. It became a European bestseller and influenced many philosophers, including John Locke.

In his *Essay Concerning Human Understanding* (1690), Locke set out his stall of blank slates. He rejected Descartes' notion of innate ideas, such as knowledge of

God and natural morality. This was not, in his view, tenable. If these ideas really were innate they must be present in every mind – and clearly they are not, since some people don't believe in God, some act immorally, and some don't even seem to have a concept of morality at all (people we might now call psychopaths).

If we were not born with ideas or knowledge, where did they come from? Locke considered the mind of the newborn infant to be like a sheet of white paper on which experience wrote the text of knowledge. The operations of the mind, including 'perception, thinking, doubting, believing, reasoning, knowing and willing'

complex ideas. The mind develops its own rules, though, so the ways in which we respond to or process incoming data vary between people. Locke's model gives each individual considerable freedom and self-determination: we can all choose how to define ourselves.

The organizing mind

There is a position between the completely blank mind and the mind primed with innate, inherited knowledge. It is the theory that the mind has an organizational structure in place, and innate activities that enable it to interpret incoming information and process it in useful ways.

'Let us then suppose the mind to be, as we say, white paper, void of all characters, without any ideas; how comes it to be furnished? Whence comes it by that vast store which the busy and boundless fancy of man has painted on it with an almost endless variety? Whence has it all the materials of reason and knowledge? To this I answer, in one word, experience. In that all our knowledge is founded, and from that it ultimately derives itself. Our observation employed either about external sensible objects, or about the internal operations of our minds perceived and reflected on by ourselves, is that which supplies our understandings with all the materials of thinking. These two are the fountains of knowledge, from whence all the ideas we have, or can naturally have, do spring.'

John Locke (1704)

forge ideas and knowledge from the sensory perceptions we collect. These actions of the mind are innate, even though no mind-content is innate. The processes, or operations, are part of human nature and don't have to be learned. By operating on simple ideas, the mind comes up with

At the most basic level, we can allow that the mind 'knows' how to do its job. Even Locke concedes this degree of innate ability. After all, it is not much more than the heart 'knowing' how to pump blood. That still leaves a lot for it to learn.

Learning to know how

Some abilities might seem innate, but on testing are found still to need some sensory input to activate them. An experiment carried out by cognitive psychologists R. Held and A. Hein in 1963 demonstrated

vertical interactions through vision alone). The kittens were kept in darkness the rest of the time, with their mothers and littermates, so their only visual stimulation was in the apparatus. At the end of the trial the mobile kittens could walk with

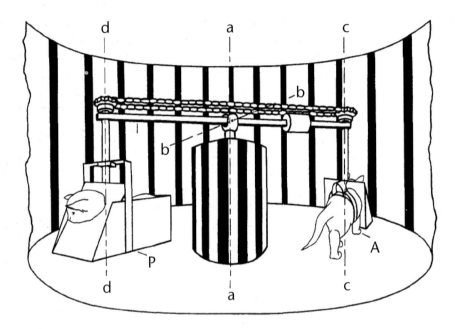

Held and Hein's 'kitten carousel'.

that we (or at least kittens) only develop true depth perception if provided with enough visual or kinetic stimulation. So, although the potential for depth perception is innate, it needs triggering.

Their experiment used pairs of kittens, put into a 'kitten carousel' for three hours a day. While in the carousel, one could move freely but the other was moved in a basket that was controlled by the movement of the other kitten. The kittens could not see each other, and the device was decorated entirely with vertical stripes (preventing horizontal/

normal paw placement but the immobile kittens could not. Held and Hein concluded that they needed self-directed movement to make sense of space.

A later study, in 1980, found that if the immobile kittens had interesting things to look at, such as moving toy cars, they did develop depth perception and were better able to walk. The combination of lack of visual stimulus and lack of self-directed movement prevented the kittens developing depth perception – either one on its own would have been enough. The second study explains why babies strapped to cradleboards in infancy, or born without limbs, are still able to develop depth perception.

A study by the Anglo–American anthropologist Colin Turnbull (1924–94) in 1961 found that humans don't develop a proper sense of perspective unless exposed to things far away and things nearby. In his study, he took BaMbuti people who usually live in dense forest in the Congo out on to the open plain. Buffaloes were grazing in the distance. A BaMbuti archer asked which type of insects they were, and would not accept that they were buffalo until driven towards them in a jeep. In the jungle he could never see more than a few metres, so had not developed the ability to relate size and distance.

Prestructured

That the mind might have structures in place to store or process particular types of knowledge, including language, was suggested by Immanuel Kant. Dissatisfied with previous explanations of the relationship between experience and reason, he set out his own theory in the *Critique of Pure Reason* (1781). As we have seen, Kant believed the mind to have 'categories of thought', which were innate mental structures or concepts that enable the mind to organize information. Categories of thought, for example, give us concepts of time and space and of causation. Simple experience, he maintained, would only ever be enough to show that one event

follows another in a chronological sequence, not that one event ever causes another. The categories of thought enable the mind to create meaning even though we are starting just from sense perceptions. Johannes Müller (1801–58) thought that his discovery of the different types of sensory nerve (see page 45 [Chapter 2: *Putting together the pieces*]) was the physiological equivalent of Kant's categories of thought. He had, he believed, found sensory input being worked upon by the nervous system before being a thought-object or perception in the conscious mind.

Immanuel Kant.

Developed in stages

The Swiss developmental psychologist Jean Piaget (1896–1980) took a distinctly Kantian, rationalistic view. He saw the child's mind as having schemata that develop slowly over time, so that the child is initially capable of largely physical interactions with the environment but develops cognitive abilities later. The schemata are formed out of building blocks of understanding. They can provide understanding of processes or objects. The newborn has some innate, inherited basic schemata that provide reflex actions. The reflex to suckle is an innate schema, for example.

As babies start to learn about the environment, they construct schemata that will help them to recognize the same events or objects the next time they encounter them. As they have new experiences, they have to adjust their existing schemata and build new schemata to accommodate new information. A child who has developed a schema to recognize a cat from a picture book, for instance, will have to adjust the schema to accommodate the size and furry feel of a cat encountered in real life. If the child encounters a new animal, he or she will need to construct a new schema to explain it. When the child can explain most events and objects, a comfortable state of equilibrium exists. If something new comes along that doesn't fit the existing schemata, disequilibrium results. The child then adjusts the schemata to accommodate the new experience, assimilates it, and returns to a state of equilibrium.

The ability to form schemata is innate, as is a sort of starter-pack of schemata for essential reflexive and instinctive behaviours.

The British psychologist Frederic Bartlett (1886–1969) further developed the idea of schemata to explain how we all process, remember and misremember information. Schemata provide a way of organizing knowledge and ideas, but they can also lead to resistance to new ideas that are hard to slot into our existing categories. Inflexible schemata lead to prejudice and to the distorting of information to fit our expectations.

Bartlett thought that these schemata were

THE WAR OF THE GHOSTS

Bartlett demonstrated the impact of schemata on memory and story-telling by telling his students a traditional North American Indian tale:

One night two young men from Egulac went down to the river to hunt seals and while they were there it became foggy and calm. Then they heard war-cries, and they thought: 'Maybe this is a war-party.' They escaped to the shore, and hid behind a log. Now canoes came up, and they heard the noise of paddles, and saw one canoe coming up to them. There were five men in the canoe, and they said:

'What do you think? We wish to take you along. We are going up the river to make war on the people.'

One of the young men said, 'I have no arrows.'

'Arrows are in the canoe,' they said.

'I will not go along. I might be killed. My relatives do not know where I have gone. But you,' he said, turning to the other, 'may go with them.'

So one of the young men went, but the other returned home.

And the warriors went on up the river to a town on the other side of Kalama. The people came down to the water and they began to fight, and many were killed. But presently the young man heard one of the warriors say, 'Quick, let us go home: that Indian has been hit.' Now he thought: 'Oh, they are ghosts.' He did not feel sick, but they said he had been shot.

So the canoes went back to Egulac and the young man went ashore to his house and made a fire. And he told everybody and said: 'Behold I accompanied the ghosts, and we went to fight. Many of our fellows were killed, and many of those who attacked us were killed. They said I was hit, and I did not feel sick.'

He told it all, and then he became quiet. When the sun rose he fell down. Something black came out of his mouth. His face became contorted. The people jumped up and cried.

He was dead.

Bartlett had his subjects recall and retell the tale several times over a year. They all thought they were retelling it accurately, but made changes such as:

- missing out information irrelevant to their lives and situations
- changing details, order and emphasis to match what seemed important to them (changing 'canoes' to 'boats', for example).

not themselves innate, but the tendency of the mind to build and populate schemata was. His experimental work included asking people to remember and repeat stories, to complete incomplete stories and to give witness accounts of events. He found that we complete stories and recall events in such ways that they accord with schemata we already have. This makes us unreliable as eye witnesses, as often we will distort what we see to fit our personal schemata and preconceptions.

Language: a special case?

Language seems to set humans apart from animals. We know of no other species with as wide a range of oral expression as we have, and we know of no human tribe or community that has not developed spoken language. That makes it a good choice for research into innate/learned behaviours.

In 1660, the French theologian and philosopher Antoine Arnauld (1612–94) and the French grammarian Claude Lancelot (1615–95) published the *Port-Royal Grammar*, which argues that grammar is a set of mental processes that are universal, so grammar is innate. A modern champion of this view is the American scientist and philosopher Noam Chomsky (b.1928) who has said that children have an innate ability to learn a spoken language. Which language they learn depends on the community in which they live, but the basic structures of all languages are universal. Learning a language is simply a matter of populating a structure that already exists in the mind with content. Chomsky maintains that language, with its very complex grammatical structure, is too difficult for a child to pick up just by imitation.

The idea that there is a universal structure or a natural organizing principle for language is supported not only by

YOU SEE WHAT YOU EXPECT TO SEE

In 1947, the American psychologists Gordon Allport (1897–1967) and Joseph Postman (1918–2004) carried out a study using a picture of a white man threatening a black man with a razor. Asked to recall and describe the picture they had seen, participants tended to say that it was the black man who had the razor. It's not just racial prejudice that leads to this kind of distortion of memory. In 1981, Cohen showed subjects a picture of a couple in a restaurant. He told some subjects that the woman was a librarian, and others that she was a waitress. When later asked to describe the woman, their accounts varied according to which job they thought the woman had.

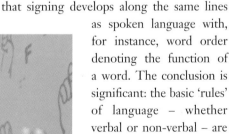

linguistic studies but by various 'experiments of nature'. These are naturally occurring situations that have given scientists the opportunity to make observations as though

THE LANGUAGE INSTINCT

The Canadian cognitive scientist Steven Pinker (b.1954) considers language to be an instinct in humans as a special adaptation, just as web-building is a special instinct in spiders. He cites the way that deaf children 'babble' with their hands and that there is a critical period for language development in children – if they don't learn to speak a language before the cut-off point they won't learn at all. This is similar to the cut-off point for vision in cats.

they were carrying out field experiments (often unethical ones).

The 'forbidden experiment' (see page 37) would no longer be allowed. But there have been various instances of non-speaking

parents, deaf or mute, raising children who are physically capable of language. Many such children learn a signing language used by their parents, but some are brought up without signed language. Of these, many develop their own way of communicating, called 'homesign', based on signs and gestures. Homesign languages were studied by American psychologists Susan Goldin-Meadow and Heidi Feldman in the 1970s. They found that homesign systems, although developed independently by isolated children or groups, share grammatical structures. This showed that language does not need to be spoken and that signing develops along the same lines as spoken language with, for instance, word order denoting the function of a word. The conclusion is significant: the basic 'rules' of language – whether verbal or non-verbal – are innate.

Starting from scratch

Whether or not we regard the newborn mind as a blank slate, there are undoubtedly some mental activities we all share. These are reflexive and instinctive behaviours. They don't require knowledge or thinking – they happen automatically. Even Locke would have to admit that the newborn suckles without being taught.

Unlearned behaviour: reflexes and instincts

A reflex action is a simple, automatic, unlearned response to a stimulus. If you pick up something unexpectedly hot, you will drop it immediately. It is the type of action that Descartes explained by reference to animal spirits flowing through the tubes that he considered the nerves to be. The instinct that makes you drop or shrink from something hot is called the withdrawal reflex, and provides an example of a reflex arc. When you accidentally touch something that is very hot, signals from

nociceptors (which detect tissue damage) travel to the spinal cord where they connect with motor nerves, triggering an automatic response, withdrawing from the source of heat. The signal from the nociceptors also travels to the brain for interpretation where it is perceived as pain. The reflex movement can start before the pain is perceived.

The newborn infant has additional reflexes (fun to play with if you have a baby to hand) such as the Moro reflex, which makes the baby spread and then unspread his or her arms rapidly. It has been suggested that the Moro reflex developed at a period in evolution when infants were carried around all day by the mother. If infants lose their balance, the reflex results in momentarily letting go and then grasping again very rapidly. It is considered to be the only innate (unlearned) fear reflex. Other reflexes of the newborn include the grasping reflex (the fingers curl around an object placed against the palm of the hand) and the rooting and sucking impulses that lead the baby to feed without instruction, demonstration or experience.

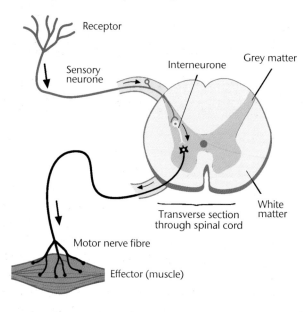

In humans, the majority of sensory neurons travel to the spinal cord rather than directly to the brain.

From reflex to volition

The English physician and philosopher David Hartley (1705–57) outlined the pattern of the child's development from unwilled reflex to voluntary, willed action and through to automatic (but willed) action. To start with, he claimed, we have involuntary

behaviours, such as the infant's grasping reflex. As children develop they learn to grasp deliberately and specifically. Babies go from instinctively grasping things to choosing which things to grasp. At this point the action has become voluntary. Associations, built up from experience, lead a child to choose to grasp a toy but not a hot coal, for instance. Eventually, the action of grasping becomes automatic again, so that we don't need to think or concentrate to grasp, we just do it when appropriate.

An instinct produces a 'fixed action pattern' (FAP). It is more complex than a reflex, which generally produces a

The moment they hatch, baby turtles instinctively head to the sea.

single action. Newly hatched sea-turtles instinctively head to the sea, for instance, and hibernating animals instinctively find and sometimes prepare a suitable place as the day length changes and the temperature drops.

It is generally impossible to suppress a reflex action, but some instincts can be suppressed. Higher animals, such as humans, can often learn the point that

triggers an instinctive action and then decide not to carry out the action. The fact that it is involuntary initially doesn't mean that it is not susceptible to volition once consciousness is applied. (There are different definitions, though: in 1961 the American social psychologists Robert Birney and Richard Teevan claimed that an instinct must be irresistible to count as an instinct.)

Instincts – behaviours you don't have to learn

Instincts were first described by the French entomologist Jean-Henri Casimir Fabre (1823–1915) whose pioneering work with insects established the field of entomology. In one of his more famous experiments, he demonstrated the power of instinct by arranging pine processionary caterpillars around the rim of a circular bowl. As the caterpillars always follow the one in front of them, they walked unceasingly around the bowl for seven days.

The first person rigorously to apply instincts to human behaviour was Wilhelm Wundt, who described any repeated behaviour as an instinct. He listed several thousand human instincts. Not long after, Freud considered behaviour in response to a natural drive – such as hunger or the impulse to reproduce – to be instinctive. By the 20th century, far fewer instinctive behaviours were being assigned to humans. The rise of the behaviourist school of psychology put much more emphasis on behaviour learned during an individual's lifetime.

Classical conditioning

With conditioning, we step outside the realm of innate behaviours and into learning. Conditioned responses, although

LORENZ'S GOSLINGS

The Austrian zoologist Konrad Lorenz (1903–89) was interested in the behaviour of birds. In a series of famous experiments, he exploited the natural instinct of greylag goslings to 'imprint' on a parent figure as soon as they hatch. Normally, this would be the mother bird. The chicks then follow the parent automatically with no further urging. Lorenz was able to show that the goslings would imprint on any nearby object – it didn't have to be a parent. He successfully imprinted goslings to follow his own boots, and they would then follow anyone who was wearing those boots. This combined the generalized instinct to imprint with an element of individual learning. In terms of the mind's structure, the activity – imprinting – is innate, but the thing-imprinted-on comes from the environment.

they are repeated responses to the same stimulus, are learned responses. The most famous example is the work of Ivan Pavlov (see page 75 [Chapter 3: *Dribble and drool*]).

This type of conditioning is known as Pavlovian or classical conditioning. It begins with a naturally linked stimulus and response pair: the unconditioned stimulus (US) and the unconditioned response (UR). There is a biological link between the two: in Pavlov's experiment the unconditioned stimulus was the smell or taste of meat and the associated unconditioned response was salivation. The experimenter links a biologically neutral stimulus, called the conditional stimulus (CS), with the US. So Pavlov's dogs came to associate a particular sound (the conditioned stimulus) with the taste or smell of meat. The conditioned stimulus then becomes linked with a conditioned response (CR) which is often (but not always) similar or identical to the unconditioned response (UR). In fact, Pavlov found that the composition of the saliva the dogs produced in response to the CS was different from that produced in response to the US.

BEHAVIOUR AND ASSOCIATIONS

When Pavlov discovered the link between conditioned stimulus and a conditioned response, he believed he had discovered the physiological mechanism that lay behind associations, and he felt it was unnecessary to look any further to discover how ideas become associated with one another.

Surprise! or not

More recent work on Pavlovian conditioning by the American experimental psychologist Robert Rescorla (b.1940) has shown that it is not as simple as it first looks. The conditional stimulus (e.g. Pavlov's bell) does not just come to stand for or replace the unconditioned stimulus (e.g. smell or taste of meat). Rather, the organism (e.g. dog) learns how the conditional stimulus fits into its environment, including its predictive association with the unconditioned stimulus. The complexity of the relationship became apparent when it was shown that if the conditional stimulus happened at other times as well as before or with the unconditioned stimulus it does not produce conditioned responses. This shows that it is the animal's learned ability to predict that is crucial to conditioning. Conditioning is, effectively, the removal of surprise from the experience. As the dog (or whatever) learns that the conditional stimulus is predictive of the unconditioned stimulus, the surprise element of the unconditioned stimulus is reduced.

Conditioned behaviour can be extinguished (made to disappear) if the conditional stimulus is presented repeatedly without the associated unconditioned stimulus. Recovery from extinction can happen if the two are associated again (re-learning the link is quicker than the original learning), or it can recur spontaneously after an interval with no exposure to the conditional stimulus.

Learning = programming

The behaviourist John B. Watson was greatly influenced by Pavlov's work. He was convinced that classic conditioning could account for all learning and behaviour, including language. In setting out his behaviourist stall in 1913, he claimed that human character could be entirely determined by careful manipulation of stimulus and response:

'Give me a dozen healthy infants, well-formed, and my own specified world to bring them up in and I'll guarantee to take any one at random and train him to become any type of specialist I might select – doctor, lawyer, artist, merchant-chief and, yes, even beggar-man and thief, regardless of his talents, penchants, tendencies, abilities, vocations and the race of his ancestors.'

In this model, heredity counts for nothing and environment is all. Further, personality is entirely determined, leaving no space for free will or even consciousness. Watson was uncompromising in his assertion that behaviour is all we have. That left him without mental structures or schemata to explain how we learn – it is simply a matter of linking a stimulus with a corresponding behaviour and reinforcing the link until it is stable.

Conditioned fear

Although impressed by Pavlov's work with dogs, Watson needed to demonstrate that it applied also to humans. He did this through the notorious and unethical 'Little Albert' experiment. In 1919, John Watson and his co-researcher Rosalie Rayner recruited a nine-month-old boy known as 'Albert' from the campus nursery. (His real name was Douglas Merritte.) They began by exposing Albert to a range of harmless objects and

animals, including a white laboratory rat. He showed no fear or adverse response to any of them – but that was about to change. When Albert touched the rat, Watson made

John Watson and Rosalie Rayner introduce Albert to a rat.

a frightening noise by striking a piece of metal with a hammer. The boy cried. He did this repeatedly until Albert cried and tried to escape when he saw the rat. Albert also became afraid of other furry white objects including a rabbit, a fur coat and a fake beard.

Unfortunately, Albert was taken away before Watson had a chance to desensitize him, so presumably the boy remained afraid of white furry things. Even more sadly, Albert died at the age of six from hydrocephalus, which he'd had since birth. As he was not (as Watson claimed) a normal, healthy boy, he was not even a suitable subject for the experiment. Critics have also complained that Watson and Rayner had only their own subjective judgments as a means of recording Albert's responses. Despite all the problems with Watson's approach, the experiment does seem to confirm that humans are susceptible to classical conditioning.

Conditioning as therapy

Making people fear white rats is not an especially useful way to use conditioning but in 1924, soon after Watson's experiment with Little Albert, the American developmental psychologist Mary Cover Jones (1897–1987) used classical conditioning therapeutically. She worked with a boy called Peter who was afraid of a white rabbit. Over a period, she exposed Peter to the rabbit, slowly bringing the two closer together until at last Peter could play happily with the rabbit and even let it nibble his fingers. Other children, who were not afraid of the rabbit, were present in the room, modelling normal responses to the rabbit. This type of behaviour therapy is still used to treat phobias.

Operant conditioning

Classical conditioning works by training a subject to associate a stimulus with a response, so they learn a behaviour through a process of association. Another type of conditioning starts from the behaviour and works backwards.

Alexander Bain (1818–1903) is often called the first British psychologist. He classed all behaviour as either reflexive or spontaneous. A reflex, as in any animal, is automatically elicited by a stimulus: if something splashes in your eye, a reflex action will close your eye. Spontaneous behaviour is initially random, but behaviours that produce a favourable response are remembered and reinforced. He was describing learning by trial and error,

Alexander Bain.

121

or 'spontaneous behavioural learning', the process B.F. Skinner would later call 'operant conditioning'.

The cat in the box

The early behaviourist psychologist Edward Thorndike (1874–1949) laid the groundwork for many later studies of learning. He used animals for his work, often cats. Thorndike devised a mechanism he called a puzzle box that could be opened from the inside by pressing a lever. The cat

was put inside the box, and a scrap of fish was placed outside to encourage the cat to escape (rather than just fall asleep, as a cat might otherwise do). As the cat explored its environment, it eventually stumbled on the lever that opened the box and then it could eat the fish. Thorndike would put the same cat back in the box several times, recording how long it took to use the lever each time. He discovered that the time decreased consistently.

Thorndike formulated the 'law of effect', which states that any behaviour that is followed by pleasant consequences is likely to be repeated, while any behaviour followed by unpleasant consequences is likely to stop. Put in everyday language – if you pick up a wasp and it stings you, you won't pick up another wasp. If you try a strawberry and it's tasty, you will probably want to eat another. The strength of the conditioning effect depends on the intensity of the response. This simple law, which looks self-evident, would form the basis of behaviourism, one of the most significant movements in 20th century psychology.

ASSOCIATIONISM AND REINFORCEMENT

The associationist model states that we form associations between elements on the basis of them occurring together (contiguity), being often in close proximity in time or space (frequency), or sometimes because they are markedly dissimilar (contrast). With Thorndike's puzzle boxes, a new model of learning emerged, known as reinforcement. This applied especially to behaviour. A behaviour is reinforced if the response is positive, encouraging the repetition of the behaviour.

Choose and be damned

The Polish neurologist Jerzy Konorski (1903–73) was the first person to thoroughly explore 'operant conditioning', as it came to be known. Konorski worked with Pavlov for two years, and originally called the new type of conditioning 'Type II' or secondary conditioned reflexes. But the name most often linked with operant conditioning is B.F. Skinner (1904–90). Skinner lived and worked in the USA, while Konorski struggled in Stalin's Soviet Union and so was outside the mainstream world of psychology. Skinner took an extreme position, which he called 'radical behaviourism', and was uncompromising in his assertion that, firstly, we have no free will and, secondly, mental events are of no real consequence in psychology. He has been called the most influential psychologist of the 20th century.

Skinner followed Thorndike in using boxes to test animal response and learning, which he then applied to human psychology. The Skinner box, as his adaptation is known, has a lever that can dispense food, but also items that can be used to produce stimuli: a light, an electrified floor grid, and a speaker. Skinner's preferred test animal was the white rat, though he also used pigeons. He tested the animals' behaviour in pressing a lever according to the responses the lever elicited, which could be positive, negative or neutral. He worked with both rewards and punishments.

When the rat knocked the lever and received a food pellet, this was positive reinforcement – the behaviour was rewarded and the rat was likely to repeat it.

If the floor was mildly electrified, making it uncomfortable for the rat, knocking the lever turned off the current. This was negative reinforcement – the behaviour removed an unpleasant stimulus – and so again the rat was likely to repeat it. Skinner trained the rats further in this. If he turned on a light shortly before turning on the electric current to the floor, the rats learned that the light was a signal and went

GAMBLING PIGEONS

In 2013, a team of researchers led by Jennifer Laude discovered that some pigeons like to gamble. The pigeons were offered two keys to peck. One key gave a large pay-out of ten food pellets 20 per cent of the time but nothing the rest of the time, while the other one always produced three pellets. The researchers discovered that some pigeons preferred the high-risk strategy. Further tests showed these to be impulsive pigeons. To test impulsivity in a pigeon, they again offered two keys, both of which paid out every time. One produced a large pay-out after a delay of 20 seconds. The other produced a small pay-out immediately. Compulsive gambling in humans follows a similar pattern and is recognized as an impulse disorder.

immediately to the lever to disable the current before it started.

As well as these ways of rewarding behaviour, Skinner also worked with punishment. A punishment may involve applying an unpleasant condition or removing a pleasant one.

It's not generally practical in everyday life to reinforce every small instance of 'good' behaviour. Skinner explored different ways of using reinforcement over time, with fixed or variable intervals between reinforcement, and fixed or variable ratios of reinforced to non-reinforced behaviour. Interval-based reinforcement schedules lead to slower behaviour. The number of acts doesn't affect the reinforcement, which comes only with passing time. This means that even the laziest subject will receive the reinforcement just by waiting. Ratio-based reinforcement schedules produce higher response rates. Since the subject doesn't know when to expect the reinforcement, they will try repeatedly – even frantically – to elicit it.

PIGEON MISSILES

The Skinner box was not Skinner's only foray into building equipment. Since boyhood, he had enjoyed making odd devices. During the Second World War, he designed a pigeon-guided missile. The nose cone of the missile was divided into three compartments, with a space for a pigeon in each. The trained pigeons would guide the missile by pecking at a picture of the target on a screen. If the pecks (and target) were not central on the screen, the pecking caused the missile's path to be adjusted. Although it was successful when demonstrated, and $25,000 of funding was allocated to it, the project was cancelled in 1944 to direct the funds to more conventional research.

Back to the mind

The behaviourist school regarded learning as a process of physical programming. That did not satisfy psychologists who had a conception of the mind. As we have seen, the Gestalt approach opposed attempts to break down mental acts, perception or experience into elements or chunks. They rejected the behaviourists' separation of stimulus and programmed response, preferring to see a pattern of learning that fitted into the whole mental state of the organism.

While Wolfgang Köhler was possibly working as a spy on Tenerife (see page 69 [Chapter 3: *Gestalt Spy*]), he was also experimenting with chimpanzees and chickens on learning. He watched the chimpanzees work out how to use tools, such as boxes, poles and sticks, to reach food that was otherwise unobtainable. He concluded that sophisticated animals learn by a system of cognitive trial and error, considering possible solutions and trying them out mentally before putting the most feasible into practice. The point at which the animal seems to have the answer is the moment of insight.

A problem, then, is either solved or unsolved, with no states in between. When insightful learning occurs, following this system, the learned result is much more mentally 'sticky' than the results of rote learning or behavioural trial and error. The insight comes from the individual's own combination of previous experiences, memories and configuration of mental fields, and it comes about as an understanding of the structure of the problem and the situation.

Chicken, in black and white

Besides chimpanzees, Köhler did a lot of work with chickens. In one experiment, he presented chickens with pieces of white and grey paper on which he had sprinkled grain. He shooed away those that wanted to eat the grain from the white paper, but allowed them to eat from the grey paper. Eventually, they all learned that they could eat from the grey sheet but not the white sheet and approached that from preference. He had successfully taught or 'conditioned' the chickens.

He then repeated the experiment with grey and black paper. A standard behaviourist model would suggest that the chickens would immediately go to the grey paper, as they had been conditioned to choose that shade. In fact, the chickens went straight to the black paper. Köhler concluded that the chickens had learned a comparison-based model: it was the darker of the two papers that held the permitted grain, not the one that was grey. The chickens, having learned a principle, applied the same principle ('eat from darker paper') to a similar situation, a process Köhler called 'transposition'.

Insights into insight

Wertheimer discovered that people learn better if they have insight. For each individual, this comes in different ways and from different sources. Consequently, there is not necessarily a single best way to learn – learning is highly individual. Memory and learning both work through a system of traces laid down by repeated personal experiences. Our recognition of, say, a cat is dependent on and informed

by all our previous encounters with cats and the memories we have of them. We each have our own concept (or schema) of 'catness' that adapts or is reinforced as time passes and we come across more cats. Although some features will be shared – the general physical appearance of a cat, for instance – other aspects will have been drawn from personal experience of individual cats. Someone who remembers a beloved pet from childhood will have a different impression of cats from someone whose predominant memory is of being attacked by a vicious cat.

Towards some theories of learning

The Gestalt psychologists had considerable influence on the cognitive school, which put discovering knowledge and constructing meaning at the centre of learning. Learning, after all, is not only about finding a way out of a maze or beginning to speak and walk – it is also about education. Cognitive psychologists saw learning as highly personal, depending on the individual's existing stock of associations and experiences, as exemplified in Bartlett and Piaget's schemata and Piaget's account of the stages of cognitive development in children (see page 128).

Even the behaviourist Edward Thorndike recognized that the subject's prior knowledge and patterns of association – or the number of stimulus-response patterns they have – can be relevant to future learning. Thorndike was

> 'If, by a miracle of mechanical ingenuity, a book could be so arranged that only to him who had done what was directed on page one would page two become visible, and so on, much that now requires personal instruction could be managed by print.'
>
> Edward Thorndike (1912)

the first to suggest that learning the Classics did not help with other areas of learning. Indeed, being adept at one subject did not help with another unless they were directly related and there were transferable skills or knowledge. He advocated learning in chunks and making the material relevant to the learner's own condition and life.

John Dewey, an educationalist as well as a psychologist, stressed the importance of making learning relevant to the student. He also said that learning materials should encourage original thought and problem solving. Piaget argued that education

PIAGET'S STAGES OF DEVELOPMENT

Birth–2 years: sensorimotor stage – learns object permanence

2–7 years: preoperational state – child is egocentric

7–10 years: concrete operational stage – understands conservation of number and volume

11+ years: formal operational stage – can manipulate ideas and engage in abstract reasoning

Before the 18th century, children were treated as smaller versions of adults. At a relatively young age, they wore adult clothes and unless they were wealthy they were expected to work. John Locke in England and Jean-Jacques Rousseau in France were the first to view childhood as a special state.

should take account of the child's cognitive development, something which he divided into clear stages (see panel). This was not entirely novel. In *Émile* (1762), the first text on the philosophy of education in the Western world, Jean-Jacques Rousseau suggested that religious education should be saved for adolescence as before this time the mind is too immature to understand the implications of religious knowledge and beliefs. What is produced in a young child is only the parroting of religious doctrine, not full understanding or faith.

Rousseau proposed that education is best achieved though exploration and discovery. He gave the example of a boy shown the shadow of a kite on the ground and asked to work out its position. The child, he suggested, should be allowed to learn through the consequences of his actions

'The noblest work in education is to make a reasoning man, and we expect to train a young child by making him reason! This is beginning at the end; this is making an instrument of a result. If children understood how to reason they would not need to be educated.'

Jean-Jacques Rousseau (1762)

(this child-centred education was intended only for boys), though his tutor would keep him safe from genuine harm. A direct line can be drawn from Rousseau to modern child-centred ideas of childrearing, taking in John Dewey and the Italian physician and educator Maria Montessori (1870–1952) on the way. (For all his influence as an advisor on childrearing, Rousseau wasn't that good a parent himself. He sent some of his children to a foundling hospital as he didn't want the bother or expense of raising them.)

Piaget saw cognitive development as being led by biology – acceleration can't be forced on the child, and attempting learning tasks that are beyond the child's stage of development is doomed to fail. He recommended learning that is active and based on discovery. The Plowden Report (1967), which set out the scheme for primary school education in the UK, was based on Piaget's research in the 1950s.

Computer memory, human memory

From the 1960s, cognitive approaches were based on the model of the computer as an information-processing mechanism. If a machine could process information and have internal states about which we can talk, why not the mind? The concept of schemata fitted well with the structure of computer data storage and manipulation. In 1968, the American psychologists Richard Atkinson (b.1929) and Richard Shiffrin (b. 1942) came up with the Atkinson–Shiffrin model of memory for the human mind. It is remarkably similar to the way in which a computer handles the input and storage of data. The model suggested three components:

The development of early computers in the 1950s and 1960s influenced the approach of many American psychologists.

- Sensory buffers: each sense organ has a buffer that receives sensory information but does not process it. The information is stored for a short while, and passed to short-term memory only if attention is paid to it.
- Short-term or working memory: this receives and holds input from both the sensory register or information retrieved from long-term memory.
- Long-term memory: this stores information indefinitely.

The sensory buffer is part of a filtering process that allows us to select which stimuli we will pay attention to. So we might take in an entire visual scene but only pay attention to something relevant, such as a threat, an item we're searching for, or a person we know.

We can, according to the American cognitive psychologist George Miller (1920–2012), keep between five and nine items in short-term memory (1956). Information in short-term memory decays and is forgotten after about 18–20 seconds unless it is rehearsed – attention is continuously or repetitively paid to it.

Information in long-term memory can be stored for a lifetime. To be attended to, it must be brought back into short-term memory. The capacity to store information in long-term memory appears to be limitless – we never stop being able to learn things. In some cases, memories become inaccessible, but they are assumed to be present: we can't remember incidents from babyhood, but they are probably stored somewhere in the brain.

Although there have been criticisms of the model since it was developed, it remains influential.

Psychobiology explains it all

Psychobiology attempts to explain the workings of the mind in terms of the physiology of the brain: chemical processes, the firing of neurons, and the physical structure of the brain.

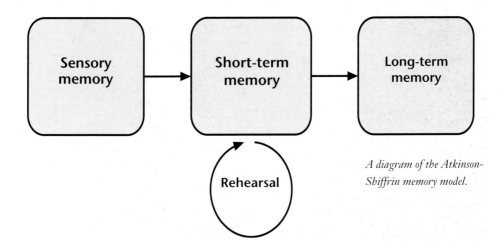

A diagram of the Atkinson-Shiffrin memory model.

The Canadian psychobiologist Donald Hebb (1904–85) set out to discover the biological processes behind association, but he soon found that nothing in the biology of the brain supported 'associationism'. Instead, he found that a new perception or a shift in attention fires a package of neurons, which he called a 'cell assembly'. For example, Hebb explained how in a child the sound of footsteps triggers a cell assembly that forms a package of perception. The next time the child hears footsteps, the same assembly is excited. If the footsteps are followed by the appearance of a parent, another cell assembly is involved in seeing the parent. The activity of a cell assembly continues for a little while, something he called reverberating neural activity. This means that if another cell assembly was activated in a very short time the two can become linked. A string of cell assemblies connected like this he called a 'phase sequence'.

So the child who hears footsteps and then sees a parent approach will form a phase sequence in which the first perception, the footsteps, automatically calls up the second before it has happened, so the child anticipates the arrival of the parent (and perhaps becomes excited) – just as Robert Rescorla found classical conditioning removes surprise (see page 119). The cell assemblies and phase sequences can be reactivated either by a genuine external perception (hearing footsteps, in the case of the child) or by an idea. This enables us to conjure up, for instance, the image of a cow when there is no cow around – the perceptions that form our idea of a cow are already linked together. The baby, according to Hebb, learns in an 'associationist' way, putting together neural connections to make cell assemblies and phase sequences. The adult, who has already made enough of these to recognize and interpret the environment, learns in a different way, largely rearranging the existing assemblies and phases through creativity and insight.

NEURON PRIMER

In 1906, the Italian physician and scientist Camillo Golgi (1843–1926) and the Spanish neuroscientist Santiago Ramón y Cajal (1852–1934) shared the Nobel Prize for Physiology or Medicine for their discovery of neurons. Neurons are nerve cells; they carry information as electrical and chemical signals to, from and within the central nervous system (CNS). Sensory neurons carry information about the environment (vision, sound, touch and so on) from the sense organs to the CNS. Motor neurons carry signals from the CNS to the muscles to control movement. Within the CNS, interneurons connect to each other within the spinal cord and brain to carry and process information.

There are many different types of neuron but typically they consist of a cell body, an axon – a long extension of the cell body up to a metre long in humans – and dendrites, which are branching ends of the axon. There can be hundreds of dendrites, allowing one neuron to connect with many others. Connections between neurons occur at synapses – tiny gaps at which chemicals carry a signal from one side to the other. The human brain has in the region of 85–100 billion neurons and perhaps a thousand times as many synapses. The model of neural networks has been copied from the brain to be applied to the design of computer systems.

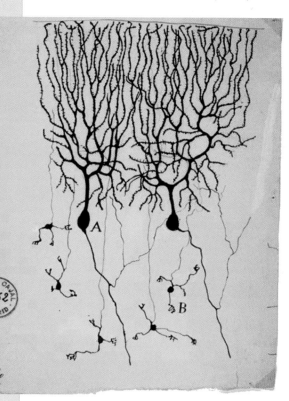

Cajal's sketches of neurons in a pigeon's brain.

131

CHAPTER 6

What makes you 'YOU'?:
defining the self

*'Many psychologists like to write the self with a capital
S, as if the self would be something precious, something
extraordinarily valuable. They go at the discovery
of the self like a treasure-digging. The self means nothing
but this thing as it is defined by otherness.'*

German psychotherapist Fritz Perls (1893–1930),
developer of Gestalt therapy

When the unfortunate astronomer David
Kinnebrooke lost his job in 1795 (see page
42 [Chapter 2: *Into the breach*]) it was because
we actually aren't all the same. His reaction
times were slower than his colleagues and
he could not change this biological fact by
any amount of effort. What makes one person
different from another, in psychological or
other aspects?

Facing page: Small Mirror Twin
by Graham Dean (2003).

Nature versus nurture

We are all different and yet we all have similarities. In particular we share similar features with our closest family. Many of us also share aspects of personality, behaviour and beliefs with our families or with larger social or cultural groups.

A central, unresolved, question in psychology asks how much of our personality, abilities and behaviour can be accounted for by nature (hereditary factors) and how much can be accounted for by nurture (the manner and environment in which we are brought up). Since the time of Locke, the *tabula rasa* model has been closely associated with the 'nurture' side of the nature v nurture debate since if

nothing is in the mind to start with, we have complete control over what a child is exposed to and so how it will develop.

Both nature and nurture can be recruited to support a highly deterministic view of personality and fate: a person could be born with criminal tendencies and so compelled genetically to do bad things, or brought up in an environment that caused him or her to develop an internal compulsion to do bad things. Studies using twins or adopted children have often been used to try to establish the level of influence that biology and upbringing have on the individual (see page 142 [this chapter: *The genetic lottery*]).

Free will and determinism

There is another question of how far an individual might be able to go in resisting these hereditary or environmental influences – whether we have free will or whether our actions are determined. The issue is further complicated when we consider that any desire or urge to resist the influence of genetics or environment is itself an aspect of character and so a product of genetics or the environment.

Whether we have any control over who we are is an important question, not just for theoretical psychology but for practical applications such as in law and education. If someone inherits a gene for psychopathy, are they responsible for their psychopathic actions? If someone's mental make-up has been forged in an environment of abuse, or stultifying prejudice, how far are they responsible for their views and behaviours?

Star-crossed

For thousands of years, people around the world have believed that our personalities are determined or influenced by the alignment of the heavenly bodies. Natal astrology – casting horoscopes depending on birth date – began around the 6th century BC, with the earliest surviving horoscope dating from 410BC. Central to natal astrology is the belief that the position of the planets and stars at a person's birth can be used as a predictor of their personality and even of events that will occur during their life. Some people still believe this. Unsurprisingly, there is no proven correlation between

A 17th-century zodiac.

personality and the position of the Earth in relation to the stars. Even so, astrology provided the earliest attempt at explaining personality.

The rise, fall and rise again of astrology

Astrology developed independently in many cultures around the world, including Babylonia, India, China and Mesoamerica. The Babylonian tradition was continued in Egypt and Greece and was carried from there to Rome. After the fall of the Roman Empire it suffered a decline in Europe but prospered in the Arab world. There was a resurgence in Europe during the Middle Ages when translations of Greek and Arab texts became available, and physicians were expected to check the astrological conditions before starting or recommending a course of treatment for patients. Even some of the great Renaissance scientists and stargazers, such as the Danish astronomer Tycho Brahe (1546–1601), the Italian polymath Galileo Galilei (1564–1642) and the German mathematician Johannes Kepler (1571–1630), were practising astrologers. They did not necessarily all believe in astrology, but it was a useful source of income.

Astrology began to lose credibility when the old model of an unchanging universe was overturned. With the discovery of comets and the confirmed appearance of new stars, the premise of astrology was thoroughly undermined. After a few attempts to shore it up, it was pretty well abandoned in the 18th century. The modern reappearance of astrology dates from a British national newspaper, the *Daily Express*, casting a horoscope for the birth of the British Princess Margaret in 1930.

In good and bad humour

For more than 2,000 years, the prevailing model of the mind and the body was rooted in the theories of Hippocrates and later Galen (see next page). They accounted for the health of mind and body, and aspects of temperament or personality, through humoral theory. Four substances, called 'humours', were thought to occur in varying proportions in the human body: blood, phlegm, yellow bile and black bile.

Six hundred years separate the ancient Greek physician Hippocrates of Cos (b.450BC) from Galen of Pergamon (AD130–200), a Greek physician living in the Roman Empire. Like Hippocrates, Galen compiled a compendium of all medical knowledge current at the time, contributing his own research and ideas. For both Hippocrates and Galen, fitness and sickness of both body and mind were controlled by the balance of the humours. When these are in their proper proportions, the body and mind are healthy. When there is an unnatural preponderance of one, or lack of one, sickness results, and health returns only once the humours are in balance.

The balance of the humours changes with diet, activity, age and lifestyle as well as with illness. In addition, each individual has a different natural temperament. Some people have a naturally high level of yellow bile, for instance, and are said to have a choleric temperament. We find them yelling at their subordinates and families, indulging in incidents of road-rage and losing their temper at the slightest inconvenience or challenge. If a person was naturally inclined to have more blood than the other humours, they would have a sanguine temperament. If a person had a preponderance of black bile, they would be of a melancholic nature. If phlegm was the dominant humour the person would be – unsurprisingly – phlegmatic.

A horoscope from 1411, showing a planet in the house of Pisces.

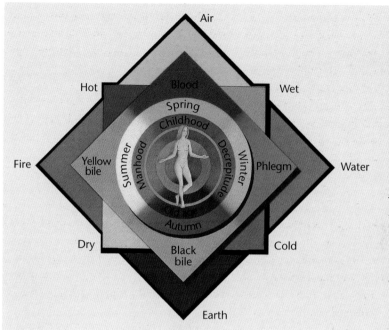

The humours were closely related to the theory of the four elements, which the ancient Greeks supposed make up all things: earth, fire, water and air. Earth was thought to predominate in black bile, fire in yellow bile, water in phlegm, and all four elements were believed to be present in blood, though with air the most significant.

Humour	Temperament	Characteristic
Phlegm	Phlegmatic	Sluggish, unemotional
Blood	Sanguine	Cheerful
Yellow bile	Choleric	Quick-tempered, fiery
Black bile	Melancholic	Sad

The humoral theory endured until the 19th century. It provided the first pseudo-biological explanation of character, and was clearly one that favoured nature over nurture, though elements of the environment such as diet or living in a damp basement could also affect the balance of the humours and so the mood.

Looks really are everything

The belief that someone's character can be read in their face has been around since ancient Greece. The idea was common in Europe during the Middle Ages, and some universities were teaching how to tell character from facial features well into the Renaissance. Not everyone accepted it, though. In England, it was eventually outlawed by Henry VIII who wanted rid of beggars and vagabonds playing 'subtile, crafty and unlawful games such as physnomye or palmestrye'. Leonardo da Vinci dismissed it as false, and without scientific foundation. On the other hand, he was prepared to accept that the lines that develop on the face with age might throw some light on character as they could indicate types of facial expression that had become habitual, such as smiling or frowning.

Humoral theory lent itself to a system

of determining character from appearance. Because the proportion of humours affected the physical as well as the mental state of an individual, it seemed likely that there would be a correlation between appearance and temperament. So the sanguine type was thought to have a ruddy appearance, and a melancholic person would look sallow and thin, for instance.

Physiognomy was revived and popularized in the 18th century by the Swiss poet and pastor Johann Kaspar Lavater (1741–1801). He believed that 'an exact relationship exists between the soul and the body'. One unfortunate consequence was his promotion of the idea that exterior beauty denotes virtue. His work was highly influential, and one of those he influenced was the German anatomist and physiologist Franz Joseph Gall (1758–1828).

Brains and bumps

Gall was the first person to distinguish between the brain's grey matter, which contains neurons, and the white matter, which contains ganglia responsible for connections within the brain. Gall was not only convinced that different areas ('organs') of the brain carry out different tasks (called localization of function) but that the shape of the skull reflected the precise structure of the brain. He thought that by measuring the bumps and lumps of the skull he could determine the size of the various 'organs' and so gain detailed insight into character. His skull-measuring came to be known as phrenology. It wasn't popular with the authorities: the church considered it anti-religious and in 1802 the Austrian

Some books on physiognomy pointed out the similarity between various human faces and animals. The individual who looked like an animal was expected also to share some features of that animal's general character.

138

PALM READING

Palmistry, chiromancy or chirognomy is the belief that a person's character and future can be discerned from the pattern of lines on the palm of the hand. It has a long history, and has been practised in China, Tibet, Persia, Sumeria, ancient Israel and Mesopotamia as well as Europe. Even Hippocrates studied patients' palms during diagnosis. Aristotle commented: 'Lines are not written into the human hand without reason. They emanate from heavenly influences and man's own individuality.' The Church suppressed palmistry in Europe during the Middle Ages, considering it a type of pagan superstition. During the Renaissance, palmistry was included along with necromancy as one of the forbidden arts. It reappeared in Europe due to the publication, in 1839, of an influential treatise on the subject by a French army officer, Captain Casimir Stanislas D'Arpentigny (b.1798), who had become interested in 'chirognomy' after a gypsy girl read his palm during a military campaign in Spain. It became increasingly popular during the second half of the 19th century.

'There are four temperaments...the lymphatic, the sanguine, the bilious, and the nervous...The different temperaments are indicated by external signs, which are open to observation. The first, or lymphatic, is distinguishable by a round form of the body, softness of the muscular system, repletion of the cellular tissue, fair hair, and a pale skin. It is accompanied by languid vital actions, with weakness and slowness in the circulation. The brain, as part of the system, is also slow, languid, and feeble in its action, and the mental manifestations are proportionally weak. The second or sanguine temperament, is indicated by well defined forms, moderate plumpness of person, tolerable firmness of flesh, light hair inclining to chestnut, blue eyes, and fair complexion, with ruddiness of countenance. It is marked by great activity of the bloodvessels, fondness for exercise, and an animated countenance. The brain partakes of the general state, and is vigorous and active. The fibrous (generally, but inappropriately, termed the bilious) temperament; is recognised by black hair, dark skin, moderate fulness and much firmness of flesh, with harshly expressed outline of the person. The functions partake of great energy of action, which extends to the brain; and the countenance, in consequence, shews strong, marked, and decided features. The nervous temperament is recognised by fine thin hair, thin skin, small thin muscles, quickness in muscular motion, paleness of countenance, and often delicate health. The whole nervous system, including the brain, is predominantly active and energetic, and the mental manifestations are proportionally vivacious and powerful.'

The English science writer and lecturer William Mattieu Williams (1820–92),
in *A Vindication of Phrenology* (1894, published posthumously)

Lavater's depiction of different temperaments in physiognomy.

DARWIN'S LAZY NOSE

Physiognomy was taken seriously. The English naturalist Charles Darwin (1809–82) almost missed out on the voyage that inspired his theory of evolution because the ship's captain, Robert FitzRoy (1805–65), a keen physiognomist, very nearly rejected him for the post of ship's naturalist out of hand. He thought the shape of Darwin's nose suggested a lack of determination.

government banned his lectures. Three years later he was forced to flee the country.

Johann Gaspar Spurzheim (1776–1832), who worked first as Gall's assistant, developed phrenology further and popularized it in America. Influential authors such as Walt Whitman, Edgar Allan Poe, Mark Twain and Herman Melville in America, and Emily Brontë and Charles Dickens in Britain, took the subject seriously and used it in their books, reflecting and boosting its popular appeal.

The study of physiognomy and

What did Kaspar Lavater's distinctive, rather spiky, profile say about his personality?

phrenology was carried out by Caucasian scientists who tended to discriminate along racial lines, unfortunately, regarding other face and head shapes as indicative of lower moral standards and meaner intelligence.

Born criminals

The Italian criminologist Cesare Lombroso (1835–1909) combined aspects of social Darwinism (see right), psychology and physiognomy in his theory of the criminal 'type'. He regarded criminality, at least in the case of serious or persistent felons, to be a matter of heredity and thought criminals represented throwbacks to early stages of human evolution. He believed criminals could be identified by 'ape-like' physical characteristics such as a sloping forehead, long arms, and a projecting jaw. Unusually sized ears and an asymmetrical face or head were also considered common characteristics of criminals. Not all distinguishing features were immediately visible: he thought that criminal types had especially acute sight, decreased capacity for feeling pain, lack of remorse or moral sense, and a propensity for cruelty, vanity, impulsiveness and vindictiveness. Perhaps some of the last features – cruelty, impulsiveness and vindictiveness – are relevant to a life of violent crime,

but the size of the ears seems an unlikely indicator of criminality. Lombroso's theory found little support in Europe but was highly influential in the United States, where it led to the idea of criminal physiognomy.

Social Darwinism

If humours and the inherited strengths and weaknesses of the brain predisposed individuals to behave in a certain way, this suggested they were strongly influenced by inherited characteristics beyond their control. This was a powerful current of thinking in the second half of the 19th

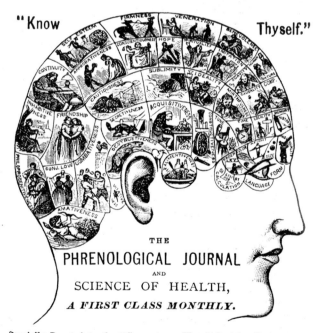

"Know Thyself."

THE
PHRENOLOGICAL JOURNAL
AND
SCIENCE OF HEALTH,
A FIRST CLASS MONTHLY.

Specially Devoted to the "SCIENCE OF MAN." Contains PHRENOLOGY and PHYSIOGNOMY, with all the SIGNS of CHARACTER, and how to read them;" ETHNOLOGY, or the Natural History of Man in all his relations

An early 19th-century phrenological map of the brain.

century, when the influence of Darwin's theory of evolution was being felt through all aspects of science. The impact on the burgeoning field of psychology was considerable. The British psychologist Francis Galton (1822–1911), famous for his work on intelligence testing and notorious for his recommendation that the less intelligent should be discouraged from breeding, coined the term 'nature against nurture'. He came down heavily on the side of nature, supporting his case with findings from his studies of monozygotic (identical) and dizygotic (non-identical) twins.

Galton and others attempted to extend Darwin's principle of natural selection to the realm of society, an approach now labelled Social Darwinism. It covers any belief that the 'better' people will thrive and the 'weaker' will or should go to the wall. It can be manifested in a *laissez-faire* capitalist system in which the sick, weak or disabled are given no financial or social support. It also gave rise to the policy of eugenics, which aimed to 'improve humanity' by curtailing reproduction among those groups considered to be detrimental to the gene pool – such as the chronic sick, disabled, mentally ill, homosexuals and some racial groups.

The genetic lottery

Since the publication of Darwin's theory of evolution and the work of Gregor Mendel (1822–84) in establishing the mechanics of hereditary characteristics, it has become generally accepted that many of our personal attributes are inherited. It is easier to see heredity at work in easily

Lombroso's criminal types

FICTIONAL CRIMINALS

The assumption that a person's criminal nature is reflected in their appearance is found in 19th-century fiction. Charles Dickens describes the criminal Fagin in *Oliver Twist* as 'a very old shrivelled Jew, whose villanous-looking and repulsive face was obscured by a quantity of matted red hair'. When he gives a first account of the convict Magwitch in *Great Expectations*, though, he does not refer at all to his personal appearance, only to his clothes and physical state, for Magwitch will turn out to be benign:

'A fearful man, all in coarse grey, with a great iron on his leg. A man with no hat, and with broken shoes, and with an old rag tied round his head. A man who had been soaked in water, and smothered in mud, and lamed by stones, and cut by flints, and stung by nettles, and torn by briars; who limped, and shivered, and glared, and growled; and whose teeth chattered in his head as he seized me by the chin.'

quantifiable physical characteristics such as eye colour and nose shape than in mental attributes, though. We all have personal experience of people who seem to share psychological features with their parents and perhaps their siblings. But how much is, say, bad temper the result of heredity and how much is due to being raised in a household of bad-tempered people? It's difficult to disentangle the roles of heredity and environment on the development of character and intelligence.

Twin studies

One way of trying to determine how much of personality is inherited – and so due to

SMILE, PLEASE – OR DON'T

Photography played a role in the development of physiognomy as a means of classifying mental type. Its rise in the 19th century meant that those working in asylums could (and did) photograph patients of all types and in different stages or states of illness and health. This provided a far larger bank of examples and wider access to them than sketches could offer. Lombroso and Galton both used photographs to establish criminal and psychological 'types', and the neurologist Jean-Martin Charcot photographed the patients he hypnotized to demonstrate stages of hysteria.

nature – is through the study of identical twins. The first twin studies were carried out by Francis Galton in the 1870s. He used questionnaires to assess psychological traits, and came down heavily on the side of nature (inherited characteristics) as being the most influential. The behaviourist Edward Thorndike conducted the first experimental twin studies, using 50 pairs of twins. He tested pairs of twins at different ages (9–10 years and 13–14 years). His results suggested that the importance of heredity decreases with age – so twins might begin with the same genetic inheritance and the same environment, but as they develop autonomy and have separate experiences, their characters diverge. The implication that both heredity and genetics affect character has been borne out by subsequent studies.

The case of intelligence

The hereditability of intelligence has proved a politically difficult subject. Galton was unperturbed by sensibilities and was happy not only to investigate the subject but to suggest that those of weak intelligence should 'find a welcome refuge' in celibate lives in monasteries rather than pass on their defective genes. He carried out the first study of genius, using a method he designed called 'historiometry', to determine whether intelligence is inherited. This used various types of biographical records to count the number of eminent relatives an individual had and to infer from that the hereditary patterns of intelligence. He found that the closer he kept to a straight line of descent (parent–child), the more likely he was to find a connection between

eminence and heredity. The method depends on the intelligent person choosing (or having access) to a field of work that allowed eminence to shine forth. His results suggested that intelligence is inherited, but shed no light on the impact of environment on realizing potential intelligence.

Although intelligence testing was a growth area – and big business – in the first half of the 20th century, the suggestion that there might be a significant genetic component to intelligence became politically sensitive during the second half of the century. If some people are genuinely less intelligent than others in a way that can't be helped – because they are born that way – there are

Twins: Kate and Grace Hoare (1879) by John Everett Millais. The sisters are identical, but Millais manages to convey their markedly different personalities.

NATURE AND NURTURE IN TWINS

Monozygotic (identical) twins are especially useful for research purposes if they have been separated from birth and raised by different families. They then have an identical genetic make-up, but different environmental influences. By comparing them, it's possible to theorize about which characteristics are the result of genetics and which are the result of environmental factors. Twins don't have to be separated at birth to be interesting, though. A study of schizophrenia in identical twins showed that in only 50 per cent of cases are both twins affected. Schizophrenia is not then entirely genetic, otherwise if one identical twin had the condition the other would too.

tricky implications for education and for the meritocratic model of society. Studies in the late 20th and early 21st century have found that intelligence is constructed from both inherited and environmental influences working together. It's what common sense would lead us to expect: someone may be born with the potential to succeed in something, but that potential can be realized or wasted depending on their home environment and the opportunities they receive in childhood.

Building 'you'

While some philosophers and psychologists have held nature to be largely or entirely responsible for personality, many others have made nurture – upbringing and other environmental factors – to be wholly or partially responsible.

Early environmentalists

Locke, who believed that the mind is a blank slate (a *tabula rasa*) and so nothing is

DEFINING INTELLIGENCE

'A very general mental capability that, among other things, involves the ability to reason, plan, solve problems, think abstractly, comprehend complex ideas, learn quickly and learn from experience. It is not merely book learning, a narrow academic skill, or test-taking smarts. Rather, it reflects a broader and deeper capability for comprehending our surroundings—"catching on," "making sense" of things, or "figuring out" what to do.'

American educational psychologist Linda S. Gottfredson (b.1947)

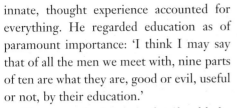
innate, thought experience accounted for everything. He regarded education as of paramount importance: 'I think I may say that of all the men we meet with, nine parts of ten are what they are, good or evil, useful or not, by their education.'

He warned that people should be especially careful about the ideas and stimuli young children are exposed to as the first marks made on the blank slate are very important: 'The little and almost insensible impressions on our tender infancies have very important and lasting consequences.' He advised against letting anyone tell the child scary stories of goblins and the like for fear of making the child afraid of the dark, for example.

Jean-Jacques Rousseau disagreed with Locke on the *tabula rasa* issue: he considered humankind to be naturally noble and good, and so had innate qualities of mind. He saw the impact of the environment and experience generally laying waste to the potential of the small, noble mind: 'Everything is good as it leaves the hands of the Author of things; everything degenerates in the hands of man.'

David Hume, a contemporary of Rousseau, went for a middle path. He saw all humans governed by passions, and of course we are all subject to the same passions, though in different degrees. The

László Polgár and family.

CHILD PRODIGIES

In a series of studies in the early 21st century, L.R. Vandervert used a brain imaging technique called positron emission tomography (PET) scanning to examine the brain activity of child prodigies. He found that some parts of the brain of gifted people (those areas relevant to their particular skill) are better developed than in the less gifted. In particular, they made more use of long-term memory. Chess teacher László Polgár set out to raise his three daughters as world-class chess players and succeeded, although as he clearly had a talent for chess, heredity can not be ruled out as an important factor. The German composer George Frideric Handel (1685–1759) had innate musical talent that thrived despite his home environment. Although he was not encouraged to play music by his parents – indeed, it was actively opposed – he emerged as an accomplished musician:

'He had discovered such a strong propensity to Music, that his father who always intended him for the study of the Civil Law, had reason to be alarmed. He strictly forbade him to meddle with any musical instrument but Handel found means to get a little clavichord privately convey'd to a room at the top of the house. To this room he constantly stole when the family was asleep.'

Handel's first biographer, John Mainwaring (1760)

MEASURING INTELLIGENCE

Francis Galton (1822–1911) was the first to test intelligence. He favoured nature over nurture in producing intelligence. In 1865 he suggested giving evolution a helping hand through selective breeding, which he named 'eugenics'.

Alfred Binet and Theodore Simon developed better, intellect-based testing in 1905. The Binet–Simon scale of intelligence rated their subjects against the normal level of skills for their age. In 1911, William Stern divided intellectual age as revealed by the Binet–Simon tests by chronological age. In 1916, Lewis Terman multiplied Stern's figures by 100 to give the now-familiar IQ (intelligence quotient) scale:

$$IQ = \frac{\text{Intellectual age}}{\text{Chronological age}} \times 100$$

different patterns to our passions define the starting points for our character. However, we all have different experiences. What we encounter in life, coupled with our individual mix of passions (character), determines what we learn and so how we will respond to future events. Previous experience and personality then construct our lives.

The parts of 'you'

The earliest experimental psychologists were not interested in how one person differs from another. Wundt and his immediate successors were more interested in the mind and its processes in the abstract than in the components of personality. The 'self' exploded on to the scene with the work of Sigmund Freud in the 1890s. His account of the three parts of the psyche, the id, ego and superego, had two parts that were innate (the id and the ego) but one part that was built up during childhood. The values of the superego are culturally determined, so the impact of the environment and experience is paramount.

According to Freud, we all share basic drives (libido), which are represented by the id. How far we follow these drives is determined by the ego balancing them against the rules the superego has developed over the individual's lifetime. Where there is conflict a drive might be repressed, forcing the discomfort experienced into the subconscious where it can do damage. Invariably, Freud found it to be an aspect of sexual drive or experience that caused problems with character.

For Freud, the unconscious was king in the province of the mind. Because, by its very nature, we can't examine the unconscious directly, we need to look for other ways to access it. One way was through dreams, another through the free association practised in psychoanalysis (see page 189 [Chapter 8: *All in the mind*]). Freud's view is highly deterministic, with early experiences causing certain predictable outcomes in terms of character (and neurosis) in adulthood.

Circles of ego and self

Carl Jung, originally an enthusiastic supporter of Freud, parted company with him over Freud's extreme emphasis on sexual aspects as the determinant of all aspects of character. Jung depicted the self as a circle, with the ego a smaller circle inside it. The self includes all aspects of personality, including the conscious and unconscious minds and the ego. The first part of one's life is spent developing the ego, building oneself through a process of differentiation. Clearly, environmental factors are paramount in the self one constructs.

The second half of life involves a return to the self, now from a position of being firmly rooted in the external world, to discover and accept one's character. It is often prompted by some kind of catastrophe or psychic wounding brought about by events (external factors). Jung's psychology often has a spiritual or mystical flavour, and this redefining of the self in the second half of life involves integration with or recognition of archetypes: 'The Self... embraces ego-consciousness, shadow, anima, and collective unconscious in indeterminable extension. As a totality, the self is a *coincidentia oppositorum*; it is therefore bright and dark and yet neither.'

Put more simply, 'The Self is the total, timeless man...who stands for the mutual integration of conscious and unconscious.' Jung saw this 'total man' as being represented in many images, including that of Christ. The goal of totality and of the consolidation and acceptance of the self would be recalled in Abraham Maslow's humanistic psychology and his focus on self-actualization (see page 157 [this chapter]).

The Austrian psychiatrist Alfred Adler (1870–1937) was the first of the Vienna Psychoanalytic Society to break away from Freud. He believed the self should be considered a unified whole, rejecting the split into id, ego and superego as unhelpful. For Adler, the individual was connected to a surrounding world and his brand of psychology was accordingly called 'individual psychology'. Freud considered his views 'honourable errors' and insisted that other members of the Vienna Society either reject Adler's theories or leave. Adler was to become highly influential, making strides in psychoanalysis that the Freudians would not match for many decades. Adler contended that external events and influences were as important as the internal

Psychiatrist Carl Jung.

struggles that Freud put at the heart of his model of psychic development. Further, Adler considered other powerful dynamics, including gender and politics, to be just as important as libido.

Adler put the inferiority complex at the heart of his psychology, finding that feelings of inferiority instilled or absorbed in childhood can have a lasting negative effect. If the individual develops a sense of inferiority, there will be an internal struggle for power that can be expressed externally in aggressive, arrogant and overly power-grabbing behaviour in compensation.

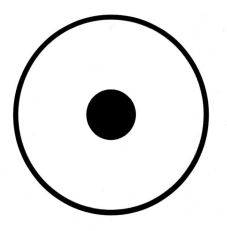

A representation of 'the self' in Jungian psychology.

In keeping with his belief that the relationship between a child and the surrounding family and wider society create the child's feelings of power or impotence, Adler advocated a style of childrearing that steered a middle path between pampering on the one side and neglect on the other and so enabled the child to develop a healthy level of self-regard. He not only dealt with the inferiority issues of adult patients in analysis sessions, but also ran sessions with parents, teachers and social workers. He encouraged them to deal democratically with children, enabling their charges to exercise power in decision-making while also learning cooperation. He taught that this prevents feelings of superiority or inferiority and the associated compensatory behaviours that cause problems in later life.

Adler was the first to promote the view that analyst and patient are equal partners in a conversation. He also advocated the need for female analysts. He believed the gender dynamic in 19th-century society was harmful for women. He was also the first to consider the influence of 'birth order' on personality. For example, he expected the eldest child to suffer feelings of 'dethronement' when younger siblings come along and they were no longer the centre of their parents' attention. At the other end of the scale, he believed that the youngest would be overindulged. Therefore the middle child or children were likely to be the most balanced, as they had experienced neither of these fates.

Adler's view was not entirely deterministic. Although he believed the individual's experiences as a child would mould their later life as an adult, he also stressed that we are free to create what we will from the experiences we have gained, though it requires conscious effort. Even bad experiences can be put to constructive use by the 'creative self': 'We do not suffer the shock of [traumas], we make out of them what suits our purposes.' We make our own beliefs and then live as if they are true, hence forging our own identities and lives, even in the face of adversity.

All around you

What is this 'environment' that has such an impact on character formation? It is everything around us. Primarily, for the infant, it is the family. For the behaviourists, who didn't believe in any inherited mental content, the impact of the environment on behaviour was all there was. As John B. Watson put it,

'All of the weaknesses, reserves, fears, cautions, and inferiorities of our parents are stamped into us with sledge hammer blows.'

With this degree of power in the hands of 'ignorant' parents, the developmental psychologists felt they had a huge responsibility to explain how to wield it.

Stamping out individuality

The American psychologist and educator Granville Stanley Hall (1844–1924) was an important pioneer in educational psychology, but his aim was not to develop the individual potential of a child but rather to mould them into a useful member of society. He considered the cult of the

---

STYLE OF LIFE

Adler saw the impact of the child's construction of power relationships manifest later in the adult's 'style of life'. By this he meant how well an individual tackles the main tasks of life, which he saw as friendship, work and love. The individual's approach, fixed by early experiences and the person's own creation of themselves, could only be altered by in-depth psychoanalysis. He identified four main styles of life, which include not just the practicalities of living but the concept of self in relation to others. All but the last of the four types are dysfunctional in one way or another:

- Ruling type: aggressive, dominating people who don't have much social interest or cultural perception.
- Getting type: dependent people who take rather than give.
- Avoiding type: people who try to escape life's problems and take little part in socially constructive activity.
- Socially useful type: people who take great interest in others and engage in a lot of social activity.

this did not give him a very tolerant view of children. He felt that reasoning with children was time wasted, and instead it was better to go for wholesale indoctrination, leading them to fear God, obey authority and develop strong bodies, all helped along with a good dose of corporal punishment.

As a child reaches adolescence, G. Stanley Hall believed, a note of altruism replaces their inherent selfishness and so it becomes appropriate to inculcate patriotism, military obedience, love of authority, awe at nature and selfless devotion to God and state. He didn't see any point in schools striving towards intellectual attainment, as the last thing he wanted to see in American youth was any individuality that might lead to independent thought or the questioning of authority. He referred to the 'storm and stress' of adolescence, and advised that the sexes be separately educated then, both to avoid distraction and so that each could be guided towards their natural

individual iniquitous and misguided, and thought it threatened to destroy America. His attitude towards childrearing was akin to beast-taming.

Hall was influenced by Darwin's theory of evolution by natural selection and also by the theory of 'recapitulation' proposed by the German biologist and philosopher Ernst Haeckel (1834–1919), which states that in its embryonic stages an organism recalls all the stages of the organism's evolutionary development. (For example, the human embryo at one point resembles a fish, and so we can deduce that humans had a fish-like ancestor.) Hall believed that in growing from babyhood to adulthood, we replay the psychologies of different stages of human evolution, starting as savages. Unsurprisingly,

> 'If there be an order in which the human race has mastered its various kinds of knowledge, there will arise in every child an aptitude to acquire these kinds of knowledge in the same order... Education is a repetition of civilization in little.'
>
> English sociologist and philosopher Herbert Spencer (1861)

roles. He strongly disapproved of having an only child, saying that, 'being an only child is a disease in itself'. In 1896 he supervised a study of only children that found them largely to be maladjusted misfits.

Hall occupies an important position both in originating the study of developmental psychology from infancy to old age (he wrote an influential text on the psychology of ageing) but also, in bringing Darwinism into psychology, in establishing the functionalist school.

Seen and not heard

Hall's attitude was not unusual at the time. In the late 19th and early 20th centuries, the general attitude towards children was that they should be strictly disciplined, never indulged and largely just endured until they could grow into useful citizens. The views of the behaviourist psychologist John B. Watson were both typical and influential. His advice on childcare was still current into the 1950s:

'Never hug and kiss them, never let them sit in your lap. If you must, kiss them once on the forehead when they say goodnight. Shake hands with them in the morning…When you are tempted to pet your child remember that mother love is a dangerous instrument. An instrument which may inflict a never-healing wound, a wound which may make infancy unhappy, adolescence a nightmare, an instrument which may wreck your adult son or daughter's vocational future and their chances for marital happiness.'

Since the behaviourists believed that all behaviour has been formed by conditioning of one form or another (classical or

'All that rot they teach to children about the little raindrop fairies with their buckets washing down the window panes must go. We need less sentimentality and more spanking.'
G. Stanley Hall

operant), and we are only the sum of our behaviours, they made the environment and our experience of it entirely responsible for who we are. Accordingly, Watson was confident that we can make anything we want of people – psychologists can become social engineers.

Defending parental love

It was against the background of Hall's and Watson's attitudes to parenting, and the prevailing view that the maternal bond with the child hinges on nutrition, that the British psychoanalyst John Bowlby (1907–90) and the American psychiatrist Harry Harlow (see page 154) carried out their work on the mother–child relationship.

Bowlby was particularly interested in the way family relationships could lead to either well-adjusted or maladjusted children and adults. He found that secure attachment, manifested in a strong bond between mother and infant, is essential to the psychological well-being of a child. This was the exact opposite of Watson's view. Bowlby was influenced by Lorenz's work on imprinting (see page 118 [Chapter 5: *Lorenz's goslings*]) to explore instinctive behaviour in babies. He concluded that the infant has an instinctive drive to form a close primary bond with one attachment figure (though more bonds are possible).

The child has innate behaviours such as crying and smiling that encourage the caregiver to interact and stay close to the child. The behaviour of the caregiver is also innate. Failure to form such a bond can lead to both psychological and physiological problems including aggression, failure to flourish, reduced intelligence, depression – and even 'affectionless psychopathy' (characterized by an inability to show concern or affection for others, and a tendency to act selfishly with no regard for the consequences of one's actions on anyone else).

Through laboratory experiments, Bowlby found that if a child is separated from the primary attachment figure (usually the mother) for a short period, he or she will become distressed. If the separation continues, they will appear seemingly calmer, but actually become withdrawn and uninterested in anything. If it continues even longer they will begin to interact with others, but will reject the caregiver and show anger on their return. He listed the stages as protest, despair and depression. His advice, in 1951, was that the child should have continuous care from the primary attachment figure for the first two years of life, and should not be needlessly separated from them for the first five years. If a child fails to form a secure attachment in the first year or two, the window of opportunity closes and irreparable psychological and emotional damage is done. The idea of a critical period accords with Lorenz's findings with his goslings. The optimum period for imprinting was, Lorenz found, 12–17 hours after hatching; if the goslings were not allowed to imprint within 32 hours it was too late and it would not happen at all.

Bowlby's findings clearly have wide-

A TWO-YEAR-OLD GOES TO HOSPITAL

In 1952, Bowlby and his colleague, the Scottish psychoanalyst James Robertson (1911–88), made a short film that showed the distress a small child experiences in hospital when temporarily separated from parents. The film changed the way hospitals treated young patients, in particular changing the visiting hours to allow parents much more contact with their children. His work with the World Health Organization guided the treatment of orphaned children in the aftermath of the Second World War.

reaching effects, including the possibility that putting a child into day-care when returning to work might do the child harm. There has been subsequent criticism of Bowlby's findings. For one thing, he did not distinguish between children who failed to form an attachment in the first place and those who formed an attachment that was then broken – through illness or death of the parent, for example. He also ascribed insufficient value to other strong bonds, such as those with a second parent, grandparents and siblings.

In 1981, the child psychiatrist Michael Rutter (b.1933) distinguished between the failure to form an emotional bond (privation) and the breaking of a bond that has already formed (deprivation), regarding the former to be the more harmful.

It might not look at first as though Bowlby's work was about learning at all. He found, though, that attachment formed the bedrock of the process in which the child learns how to be a person. The child, he says, learns from the caregiver how to interact with others and also builds their model of their own identity on the basis of how the caregiver responds to them.

Bowlby's findings are largely supported by later research, with some qualification. Harry Harlow's brutal experiments on deprivation in infant monkeys (see below) and several studies involving children kept in institutions support the general view that lack of attachment leads to emotional disturbance, physical and psychological ill-health and delayed or arrested development.

Research in 1989 by the developmental psychologists Jill Hodges and Barbara Tizard with a group of children who had spent their early years in institutions found that those who were adopted at age four were able to form strong attachments with their new families and did not develop affectionless psychopathy. This later study suggests the effects need not be as dire and irreversible as Bowlby suggested, at least as long as a child is given a chance of stable affection during their early years.

Deprivation and depression

The American psychologist Harry Harlow (1905–81) also explored the 'uses' of attachment to the mother. In 1958, he was raising monkeys to use as experimental animals when he noticed that those hand-reared in isolation were psychologically different from monkeys kept with their mothers. To investigate the role of the mother, he carried out a series of (unethical) experiments that involved separating baby monkeys from their mothers and rearing some of them in isolation for up to 24

FORTY-FOUR THIEVES

Bowlby studied a group of 44 young people labelled as delinquents who were attending a clinic after being found guilty of crimes and compared them with a control group of 44 young people who were attending the clinic with non-crime-related issues. He discovered that, compared with the control group, a higher proportion of the delinquents had endured periods of separation from their mothers in early childhood and showed signs of affectionless psychopathy. He concluded that maternal deprivation led to their problems of delinquency and psychopathy. Later commentators have pointed out that although his results show correlation, causation can't be inferred. Other factors, such as diet, poverty or frequently moving house or school could also have contributed to their behaviour.

months. The isolated monkeys grew up to be extremely mentally disturbed and incapable of normal parenting themselves.

Harlow made surrogate monkey mothers from wire and wood, some covered with cloth. He put one of each type in each baby monkey's cage. One of the two was fitted with a feeding bottle. The baby monkeys all preferred the cloth mothers, whether or not they held the feeding bottle. If the wire mother had the bottle, the baby would go to it only to feed and then return to the cloth-covered mother for comfort. Each baby monkey had its own surrogate mother, and grew attached to it, learning to recognize it and preferring it to other similar ones. Baby monkeys placed in a new environment with their fabric mothers would explore their surroundings, returning frequently to the fabric mother for comfort. Baby monkeys left alone in the new environment did not explore, but showed behaviour associated with extreme distress (such as curling up and screaming).

Harlow concluded that nourishment is not the most important aspect of the mother–child bond. It had a revolutionary impact.

At around the time that Bowlby and

Harlow presents a baby monkey to a wireframe 'mother'.

Harlow were experimenting with mother-love, the American paediatrician Benjamin Spock (1903–98) published *The Common Sense Book of Baby and Child Care* (1946), which denounced the practices promoted by the behaviourists to train babies by leaving them to cry, enforcing strict feeding times and sleep routines, and withholding affection. Spock recommended that parents follow their instincts, give affection and vary their practice to suit the character of the individual child. The

book was highly influential. Later, critics of the perceived social problems of the second half of the 20th century (such as sexual liberation) put the blame squarely on Spock and his 'permissive' approach to childrearing. His detractors claimed that by encouraging indulgence, he had contributed to a generation of people with an exaggerated sense of entitlement and no moral fibre.

PIT OF DESPAIR

Harlow, suffering depression himself after the death of his wife in 1970, carried out experiments in which he kept monkeys in darkness and isolation in a tank he provocatively called the 'pit of despair'. The monkeys quickly became disturbed and depressed. He then examined their depressive state and tried to heal it:

'In our study of psychopathology, we began as sadists trying to produce abnormality. Today we are psychiatrists trying to achieve normality and equanimity.'

Some of his colleagues felt his experiments went too far – they would certainly be considered unethical today – and it has been suggested that they prompted the animal liberation movement in the US.

The Romanian orphanages

Under the rule of Nicolae Ceausescu in Romania, up to 170,000 children were kept in orphanages in abject squalor. They were subject to abuse and neglect, often kept tied to their cots, lying in their own filth, undernourished and never washed, picked up or shown affection. In 1989, a number of charities moved in to help the orphans. Psychologists were able to study the children over many years while attempts were made to rehabilitate them.

Many of the children suffered lasting physical and psychological effects. This included impaired intelligence and stunted growth (many still looked about six years old even as teenagers). They had failed to produce growth hormones, and the lack of intellectual and emotional stimulation had prevented normal development. Some of those rescued from the orphanages at a young age and placed with loving foster families made a good recovery, but for many, and especially those who had spent longer in the institutions, the damage was irreversible.

'The Child is father of the Man.'
English poet William Wordsworth
(1802)

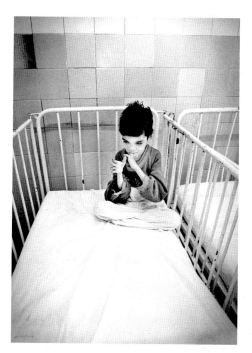

A Romanian orphan in 1989.

Becoming yourself

The humanistic psychologists of the late 20th century focused on the conscious, chosen development and perfection of the self. For them, whatever upbringing we have had, we are all in control of forging our later selves. The ultimate goal for the human was, in Abraham Maslow's term, self-actualization. It was pretty much what Aristotle had advocated 2,300 years previously.

Robbing the past of its potency

Power to make ourselves, without regard to what had gone before, was also a theme taken up by the early German-American Gestalt psychologist Kurt Lewin (1890–1947). He tried to dismantle the tendency to impose categorization on people – expecting children to reach certain landmarks in behaviour by certain ages, for instance, or classifying people as 'introvert' or 'extrovert'. He defined the individual's 'life space' – that is, the landscape of external and internal factors acting on them at any point in time that influences their behaviour. For Lewin, events in the past had no relevance unless they were recalled at the present moment. So childhood experiences (so important to Freud) would not influence someone's behaviour as an adult unless they were called to mind. Instead, he believed that our behaviour is shaped by forces that either drive us forward or inhibit our actions.

Lewin believed that needs produced tensions that the individual would try to resolve – finding food to satisfy hunger, for instance. A need would dominate the life space to a greater or lesser degree until it was resolved. Needs could be biological (such as being thirsty) or psychological (such as wanting a more stylish car). This is now called the 'Zeigarnik effect', named after the Lithuanian psychologist Bluma Zeigarnik (1901–88). Lewin delineated different types of conflict within individuals, which he summarized as:

- Approach–approach conflict: wanting each of two options and having to choose one (such as choosing between two holiday destinations).
- Avoidance–avoidance conflict: being repelled by two options but having to choose one (such as agreeing to an unpleasant surgical procedure or enduring long-term discomfort).

- Approach–avoidance conflict: both wanting and being repelled by an aspect of a single goal (such as wanting a qualification but not wanting to put in the time and effort needed to study for it).

Lewin saw behaviour as a function of the person in their environment, which he presented in scientific notation:

$B = f(P, E)$

where B is Behaviour

P is the Person

E is the Environment

It is a heuristic statement of a relationship, rather than a mathematical formula.

Will you, won't you?

One of those most influenced by Lewin was the American psychologist Leon Festinger (1919–89), who introduced the term 'cognitive dissonance'. This arises when we hold two conflicting views, or act in a way that is not in accordance with our beliefs. We can experience cognitive dissonance if we decide to get fit and then spend the weekend slobbing on the sofa, or if we think we believe all people are equally likely to be intelligent but expect lower performance from one type of person, whether it's women, Americans, the elderly, or any other disparate group.

Festinger and fellow psychologist James Merrill Carlsmith (1936–84) employed students to carry out a dull task. The participants were then paid either $1 or $20 to tell the next group of waiting students that the task was interesting. When later questioned about the task, those who were paid $20 said it was boring, but those who were paid only $1 rated it as more interesting. The researchers explained this result in terms of cognitive dissonance. The students who had been paid $20 felt they had been paid well enough for compromising themselves by lying, so they did not need to pretend to themselves that the task was more interesting than it was. But the students who had only been paid $1 either had to admit to themselves that they had lied for a small reward, or they had to change their view of the task. It was easier to admit they had been wrong in their opinion of the task than to accept that they had lied in exchange for a tiny reward.

Carlsmith undertook another study in cognitive dissonance in 1963 with fellow US psychologist Elliott Aronson (b.1932), this time using a group of young children. In each trial, a child was left in a room with lots of toys. They could play with all of them but one, which they were told was extra special. Half of the children in the group were threatened with a serious punishment if they played with the special toy. The other half were threatened with a mild punishment. None of the children disobeyed. Later, the children were allowed to play with any toy, including the special one. Those threatened with a mild punishment were less likely to play with the prohibited toy than the other children. Carlsmith and Aronson suggested the children rationalized their self-policing response to the mild threat by persuading themselves that the toy was not really interesting, so they didn't want to play with it when they were allowed to.

This recalls Piaget's account of how children adjust their schemata to accommodate new experiences or information, shifting from a state of

equilibrium to disequilibrium and then back. In the case of cognitive dissonance, it is the person's schema for him- or herself that is threatened by the mismatch between act and belief, so the schema is adjusted to accommodate the behaviour.

> 'If a person is induced to do or say something which is contrary to his private opinion, there will be a tendency for him to change his opinion so as to bring it into correspondence with what he has done or said.'
>
> Leon Festinger and J. Merrill Carlsmith

Act as you want to be

In 1972, the American social psychologist Daryl J. Bem (b.1938) proposed an alternative to cognitive dissonance that he called 'self-perception theory'. He believed that the way we judge the character of other people is to view their behaviour and infer what they are like, and he suggested that we might do the same with ourselves. It sounds counter-intuitive: it would seem more logical that our behaviour stems from our

character, rather than the other way round (although the behaviourists would disagree that we are 'like' anything). Bem adapted Festinger's 'boring task' experiment. He played a tape to two groups of subjects. Each tape gave the testimony of a man saying the task was interesting. Bem told one group that the man had been paid $20 for his testimony and told the other group that he had been paid $1. Those who thought he had been paid only $1 concluded that he really had found the task more interesting. Bem suggested that they believed he would not have given such a positive account of the task for $1 if he had not actually enjoyed it, and that in Festinger's study the same thing was happening – the subjects assumed they had enjoyed the task because they were prepared to give a positive testimonial for $1.

In other words, we interpret our own personalities from our behaviour. In that case, changing our personalities can be achieved by changing our behaviour – we are completely free to rebuild ourselves. (This recalls William James' ideas; see page 61 [Chapter 3: *The birth of American psychology*].)

Become who you want to be

More than 2,000 years ago, Aristotle considered that the aim of life was to become a whole person, living according to one's moral standards and values, and that this was the source of happiness. One could be happy, in Aristotle's terms, even in prison and when persecuted as long as one's integrity was intact. It's a view that

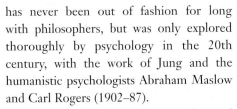
has never been out of fashion for long with philosophers, but was only explored thoroughly by psychology in the 20th century, with the work of Jung and the humanistic psychologists Abraham Maslow and Carl Rogers (1902–87).

Jung, as we have seen, saw the goal of the second half of life as consolidation and acceptance of the self, becoming a 'total [hu]man'. Indeed, he considered the point of middle age to be to achieve this state of contentment.

Maslow put this consolidation and acceptance at the pinnacle of his 'pyramid of needs' (see page 179). This sets out the needs that Maslow thought drove all human activity. At the top of his pyramid, when all other needs have been met, is the need for self-actualization. This is the process of becoming the person you want to be, of fulfilling your potential and being comfortable in your own skin. It is, necessarily, different for everyone. He was not there to judge someone's version of self-actualization, only to

promote it as the ultimate goal of human life. For one person, self-actualization might come about through being a supportive, reliable and affectionate family member. For another, it might only be achieved with a Nobel Prize, or great respect in the community.

Maslow carried out his research

The 'self-actualized' Abraham Lincoln.

'*The organism has one basic tendency and striving – to actualize, maintain, and enhance the experiencing organism.*'

Carl Rogers (1951)

into self-actualization by studying the biographies of a gallery of famous people he considered to be self-actualized, including Albert Einstein, William James, Sigmund Freud, Eleanor Roosevelt and Abraham Lincoln. Although Maslow thought that

---

HEBB'S RECTANGLE

In addressing the question of whether nature or nurture is more important in forging identity, the Canadian psychobiologist Donald Hebb (1904–85) said that the two were both involved in a way that is impossible to untangle. He likened the involvement of both nature and nurture to the involvement of both length and breadth in calculating the area of a rectangle – there is no rectangle without both, but there is a lot of variation possible within that basic model.

---

self-actualization can only be attended to after the more basic human needs have been met, evidence suggests otherwise. Many artists and spiritual leaders have achieved self-actualization despite their basic needs for food, shelter and health going unmet. Carl Rogers considered childhood experience to be the main factor in determining whether someone will eventually become self-actualized – and that many will not. Maslow agreed that most people – perhaps 98 per cent – will never achieve self-actualization. But that was their own fault. We are all, in his view, free to take the actions that will lead us to achieve self-actualization. We are all the authors of our own character.

End of the self?

Some social and cognitive psychologists in the late 20th and early 21st century have queried the validity of the concept of the self as a 'thing' at the heart of cognition, like a spider at the heart of a web. Instead the 'self' is something that emerges from overlapping cognitive processes. Self-categorization theory, developed by the British psychologist John Turner (1947–2011), suggests that we define ourselves in terms of our membership of groups, from family to the human race as a whole. In belonging to a group, we consider the similarities we share with its members, and the differences between us and members of other groups. We use identification with groups to depersonalize ourselves in some ways, according to Turner. So, if a man identifies himself as part of the army, he will stress the ways in which he is the same as other soldiers. Externally, this is shown by conforming to the requirements or expectations of the group – wearing a uniform, obeying orders and so on. Self-categorization makes the self a more fluid thing, and one that can change with time and circumstances.

Our membership of groups is at its widest in our membership of the human race. For all the psychological characteristics and processes that mark us out as individuals, there is a lot that we share with all other humans – not all of it pleasant or comfortable.

CHAPTER 7

What makes you
ONE OF US?:
the self and society

'[The] whole spiritual heritage of mankind's evolution [is] born anew in the brain structure of every individual.'

Carl Jung (1875–1961)

While our personal experiences do much to build our individual minds, there is also a good deal that is common to all people. The human condition is what unites us. Psychology is concerned as much with what unites us as the differences between us.

Facing page: *Although we like to assert individual identities for ourselves, most of us are also perfectly happy to follow the crowd.*

Nurture suppressing nature

Two philosophers who shared the view that living as part of society suppressed our basic urges and behaviour had totally opposite views of what that 'natural' human state was like. The English philosopher Thomas Hobbes (1588–1679) believed that in their natural, 'uncivilized' state humans would be driven solely by selfishness and would quickly resort to violence – life would be 'nasty, brutish and short'. However, Jean-Jacques Rousseau, writing a hundred years later, thought that natural man had an innate dignity and nobility. Neither philosopher, though, had any empirical evidence in support of the 'natural' human state he was proposing. Specific experimental research into the 'true' nature of human beings, when given freedom to act without restriction, would only emerge in the 20th century.

Our mental toolkit

Darwin influenced the development of functionalism and behaviourism by setting out that a successful organism is one that survives and reproduces. Human behaviour, like that of animals, can be investigated and

LAMARCKIAN INHERITANCE AND BAD SMELLS

Lamarck's theory of evolution through the inheritance of acquired characteristics (see page 105) was replaced by Darwin's theory of evolution by natural selection and has been largely ignored and even ridiculed for the last 150 years. But Lamarck might yet have the last laugh. Modern research into epigenetics suggests that some adaptations to the environment may indeed be passed on to the next generation. This is thought to work through changes in the epigenome, the control mechanism that regulates gene expression by turning them on or off.

Research published in 2013 by the American behavioural psychologists Brian Dias and Kerry Ressler found that when mice had been conditioned to fear a smell their offspring also responded with sensitivity and negative responses to the same smell, even though they had not themselves been conditioned to dislike it. The offspring had been produced using *in vitro* fertilization and so had had no contact with their biological parents, so could not have learned the fear from them.

explained in terms of how well any type of behaviour serves the ends of survival and reproduction. This is the subject matter of evolutionary psychology.

If the brain has evolved to be fit for purpose, to fulfil certain functions to aid the survival of both the individual and the human species, it seems to do so by equipping each child with a starter-pack of useful instincts, mental structures, processes and behaviours.

Common structures

The structuralists and functionalists both worked from the assumption that it was possible to discover aspects of the mind that were common to all people. These would pattern thought and perception, and ensure a certain degree of conformity. Darwinian evolution gave a particular impetus to functionalism, as the functions of the mind must surely be those that would make it most fit for purpose, for ensuring the survival of the individual and their reproductive success?

Recent research into disgust and fear suggests there is a strong and apparently innate disgust response to many things that herald or signify disease, including vomit, faeces, rats and cockroaches, and to animals that recall mucous or pus, such as slugs and leeches.

Whether these are the result of common mental structures and functions or part of a collective 'genetic memory' (like Jung's collective unconscious) is unclear. Genetic memory is generally disregarded by current psychologists.

We have already considered some of the ways in which the brain or mind has been thought to demonstrate common features, shared by us all. There are Jung's archetypes and collective unconscious, the propensity to build schemata and the possible special structuring of the brain/mind to make it receptive to language-learning.

The common childhood

Although Freud's method of psychoanalysis is very much concerned with personal histories and their outcomes, he drew conclusions from his cases that he applied to the human race in general. His description of the ego, superego and the id (see page 28 [Chapter 1: *The tripartite ghost revisited*]) proposes a common structure to all minds. Further, his account of how we all develop through the oral, anal and genital stages, how all children are affected by an Oedipus complex (see page 191 [Chapter 8: *Freud's problems with sex*]) and how every type of neurosis can be traced back to some type of sexual exploitation or event (real or imagined) suggests a greater degree of commonality.

It's worth remembering, though, that Freud based his conclusions about all human nature on his own recollections of childhood and what he could discover from his patients through hypnosis, free association and extensive discussion. It is a big leap to assume that the experiences of the middle classes in 19th-century Vienna can be extended to people living in very different circumstances, times and places.

Are we good or bad?

Hobbes thought natural humans would fight each other in an orgy of selfishness; Rousseau believed humans displayed nobility and dignity in their natural state. Who was right?

The legacy of the Nazis

The Holocaust was one of the most horrific crimes of the 20th century and, indeed, of all human history. In its aftermath, people around the world asked what could drive one human being to treat another the way that SS concentration camp guards had treated their victims? What had happened to ordinary German people to make them capable of such atrocities? The question was especially pertinent to social psychologists, and several famous experiments in the years after the Second World War sought to explore the state of mind that could lead to cruelty on such a mass scale. This was not an event that could be laid entirely at the feet of a few deranged individuals; it required an explanation that took account of the enormous number of perpetrators and their previously good character – their roles as ordinary workers, fathers, husbands and friends.

Crowds line the street of a Czechoslovakian town to greet a parade of Nazi troops, c.1939.

Free reign to commit harm

In 1971, the American psychologist Philip Zimbardo (b.1933) set up an experiment in Stanford University to explore the interaction between prison staff and their prisoners. He recruited healthy male volunteers who were allocated roles as either prisoner or guard. The experience was made as realistic as possible for the

A 'guard' takes part in Zimbardo's experiment.

prisoners, beginning with arrest at an antisocial hour and in full view of their neighbours. The prisoners were given dehumanizing uniforms and addressed only by number. The guards were also given a uniform, including dark glasses. The guards were allowed to use any methods they wished in order to keep the prisoners under control.

The 'prison' was an adapted corridor in the psychology department of Stanford University. The doors had steel bars, the 'exercise yard' was a corridor, and there was a converted cupboard for use as a cell for solitary confinement. Prisoners slept three to a bare cell with just enough space for their beds.

As the guards began to assert their authority, prisoners were frequently woken at night to be counted. The guards were allowed to punish prisoners and often did so by forcing them to do push-ups. Nazi concentration camp guards had done the same, and US soldiers later did so in the US military prison Abu Ghraib, in Iraq. One of Zimbardo's guards stepped on the prisoners' backs or made other prisoners do so during these push-ups.

The second day, the prisoners rebelled. The guards used fire extinguishers to drive them back, then stripped the prisoners naked and put the ringleader into solitary confinement. Soon the guards moved on to methods of psychological control. They singled out some prisoners for special treatment, then arbitrarily switched their favours, so causing disorientation, dissent and distrust within the group. A day and a half into the experiment, the first of the prisoners started to suffer mental breakdown. Yet even the experimenters were now so deeply immersed in the prison mentality that they accused him of faking his distress. It was several days before he was removed from the experiment. When the experimenters heard of a planned escape,

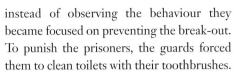

instead of observing the behaviour they became focused on preventing the break-out. To punish the prisoners, the guards forced them to clean toilets with their toothbrushes.

The study had been scheduled to last 14 days. Zimbardo called a halt to it after six, but only when visiting social psychologist Christina Maslach expressed her horror at how the prisoners were being treated. She was the only one of fifty visitors to have voiced concerns (Zimbardo married her the following year). Four of the nine prisoners had already broken down.

Zimbardo discovered three types of guard in the study. One type was tough, but treated the prisoners fairly as long as they were obedient. Another type was benevolent, doing small favours for prisoners and never punishing them. And a third type seemed to relish the power they had, finding ever more imaginative ways to hurt prisoners and abusing them when they thought they were not being observed (there were hidden cameras). There was nothing in the guards' mental profiles at the start of the experiment that Zimbardo could regard as predictive of their subsequent behaviour.

A foreshadowing of Abu Ghraib

Zimbardo has noted the similarities between his experiment and the prisoner

abuse in the US military prison Abu Ghraib. Stripping prisoners, forcing them to stand with their head covered, and making them fake humiliating sexual acts were tactics used in Stanford and Abu Ghraib. The abuse in Abu Ghraib was blamed on 'a few bad apples', but Zimbardo has argued that there are not bad apples that spoil the barrel, but rather bad barrels that spoil the apples. The situations we put people in can either make – or allow – them to do bad things.

Zimbardo's experiment seemed to uncover a dark aspect of human nature; a willingness or even an eagerness to harm

'If only there were evil people somewhere insidiously committing evil deeds, and it were necessary only to separate them from the rest of us and destroy them. But the line dividing good and evil cuts through the heart of every human being.'
Alexander Solzhenitsyn (1918–2008), *The Gulag Archipelago* (1973)

others for no good reason just because they could. He felt that anonymity aided the descent into cruelty, and the position of authority that the guards were given enabled it to happen. He noted that people quickly slipped into the roles assigned to them, so it's not possible to say whether the 'evil' guards acted out of innate evil that is usually suppressed or whether they were, at least in part, acting in the way they thought fitting for their role. Unlike the Nazi prison guards, though, no one had told them to be cruel. Where did it come from? Zimbardo has said that in these situations, past and present disappear and only the gratification of the moment counts. People do things without considering the consequences or the reasons. And no one can say that he or she would not do it. That is why it's so frightening.

'Any deed that any human being has ever committed, however horrible, is possible for any of us— under the right circumstances. That knowledge does not excuse evil; it democratizes it, sharing its blame among ordinary actors rather than declaring it the province of deviants and despots—of Them but not Us. The primary lesson of the Stanford Prison Experiment is that situations can lead us to behave in ways we would not, could not, predict possible in advance.'

Philip Zimbardo

LORD OF THE FLIES

The novel *Lord of the Flies* (1954) by William Golding takes as its premise the question of how people would act if liberated from the strictures and observation of society. It takes the situation of a group of young boys stranded without adults on an island and shows them descending into anarchy and cruelty. Golding took Hobbes' view of the natural 'bestial' nature of humankind. Zimbardo's experiment seemed to endorse it.

Things turn nasty on the island in a still from Peter Brook's 1963 film adaptation of Lord of the Flies.

A happier possibility

Paul Bloom (b.1963) is a cognitive psychologist at Yale University. His experiments with babies as young as three months suggest that we might have an innate moral sense that leads us to prefer altruistic behaviour to obstructive and selfish behaviour. In working with very young children, direction and duration of gaze is used to indicate interest or preference. Bloom showed the babies an animation of a ball trying to go up a hill, then of a helpful square nudging it upwards and of an unhelpful triangle blocking its path. The babies greatly preferred the helpful square shape. He changed the helpful/unhelpful shapes and their colours to rule out aesthetic preference. He found that adding faces to the shapes strengthened the effect. Even the smallest babies preferred the helpful shapes, and they were too young to have learned about considerate and inconsiderate behaviour, so Bloom concluded that this showed an innate rudimentary moral sense.

The children in a 1961 study by the Canadian social psychologist Albert Bandura (b.1925) were old enough to know the difference between good and bad behaviour. He wanted to know whether they would follow a role model, good or bad, given the opportunity to do so, without risk of punishment. He and his colleagues at Stanford recruited 72 young children, with adult researchers to act as models, and acquired some Bobo dolls – large, durable inflatable dolls that can be knocked over but quickly spring back to an upright position.

He divided his 72 young subjects into groups who were exposed either to an adult behaving violently towards a Bobo doll, a non-aggressive role model who played normally with some toys, or no role model. The children later had unsupervised access to the Bobo doll.

Bandura found that children who had seen an aggressive role model were the most likely to abuse the Bobo doll themselves.

DARWIN'S BABY

Charles Darwin made detailed notes on the development of his son, William. He recorded that at two years and eight months, his son showed signs of guilt and shame, hiding the stains on his clothes that showed he had stolen food. Darwin reported that the boy had never been punished, so he was not motivated by fear of the consequences.

Darwin and William, c.1842.

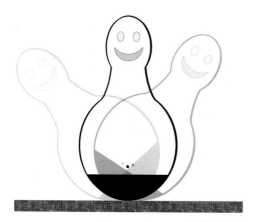

The least aggressive children were those exposed to a non-aggressive role model, so that seemed to have a good influence (better than no role model at all). Seeing a male aggressive model was more likely to make boys aggressive; the gender of the role model made little difference to girls, except that if they saw a male aggressive role model the girls were more likely to be physically aggressive and if they saw a female aggressive role model they were more likely to be verbally aggressive.

There have been criticisms of the experiment. Would the effect have lasted longer than the few minutes of the experiment? Were the children trying to please the adults by copying their behaviour?

Bandura carried out a similar experiment in 1963 with children aged between two-and-a-half and six years old. He showed the children films in which a model aggressively attacked and screamed at a Bobo doll, and then was either rewarded with sweets, or punished with a warning. The children were then allowed to play in a room with a Bobo doll. Children who had seen the aggression rewarded were more likely to be aggressive themselves.

Variations on the Bobo doll experiment have consistently come up with much the same results. Modern brain scanning methods can add a physiological dimension to such experiments. In 2006, a study at the Indiana University School of Medicine carried out brain scans on 44 young people straight after they had played either a violent or a non-violent video game. Those who had played violent games showed extra activity in the amygdala, the part of the brain responsible for stimulating emotions. There was reduced activity in the prefrontal lobe, which regulates self-control, inhibition and concentration. Those who played non-violent games showed no such changes in brain activity. Studies such as this, showing a change in behaviour and brain activity common to several subjects, suggest there is a genuine mechanism at work in the mind that could be predictive of behaviour and might well be common to all people.

Follow the crowd

Most of us want to fit in to society to varying degrees. Even if we don't consciously want to conform, we quickly learn that life is a lot easier if we observe some social norms. A series of experiments in the mid-20th century explored the degree to which people want to conform, obey, fit in and generally not rock the boat. People are, it seems, more compliant and timid than we expect.

Doing as you're told

Fitting in can sometimes be good, but it can also lead to very bad behaviour – as in the case of the Nazi atrocities. Another of the experiments that followed in the wake

'Sit Down You're Rockin the Boat!' So Stubby Kaye's character is advised in Guys and Dolls *(1955). Most of us, it would seem, are happy to conform to social norms.*

of the Second World War tested subjects' willingness to follow orders, even when those orders were to behave in unacceptable ways. Its results were shocking.

The Milgram experiment

In 1961, the American social psychologist Stanley Milgram (1933–84) recruited 40 volunteers to help with a study of learning at Yale, all of them men between the ages of 20 and 50 (so comparable to those who might have become concentration camp guards in Nazi Germany). He told them they would be randomly allocated roles as learners or teachers, but in fact they were all to be teachers and the 'students' were actors.

The 'teacher's' role was to ask questions of a 'student' seemingly strapped to a chair in another room and attached to two electrodes. He was told that if the student got a question wrong, he was to administer an electric shock. This started at a very mild level of 15 volts, but rose progressively to a

> 'When you think of the long and gloomy history of man, you will find more hideous crimes have been committed in the name of obedience than have ever been committed in the name of rebellion.'
>
> B.F. Skinner (1974)

'Could it be that Eichmann and his million accomplices in the Holocaust were just following orders? Could we call them all accomplices?'

Stanley Milgram (1974)

maximum of 450 volts as the student gave more and more incorrect answers.

The teachers were given a script to follow, and strict instructions to administer shocks for wrong answers or silence. The student also had a script, and had to act out screaming, begging and writhing in their chairs as they were apparently subjected to more and more pain. At 300 volts, the student banged on the wall, begging to be let out; at higher levels of shock the student fell silent. The experimenter sat in the room with the teacher and encouraged him to carry on if he became reluctant. The teacher could hear but not see what was happening in the other room. The experimenter would urge the teacher to continue with the experiment but did not threaten or intimidate in any way.

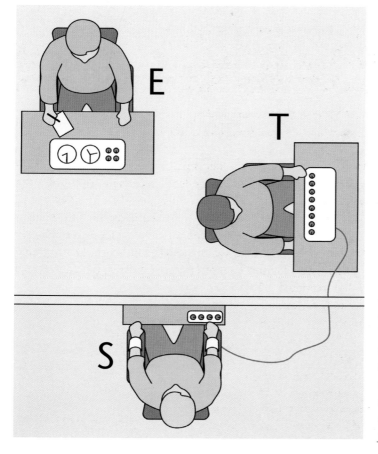

A diagram of the Milgram experiment. The experimenter ('E') tells the teacher ('T') to administer a set of electric shocks to the student ('S'), who is actually an actor reading from a script.

'I set up a simple experiment at Yale University to test how much pain an ordinary citizen would inflict on another person simply because he was ordered to by an experimental scientist. Stark authority was pitted against the subjects' strongest moral imperatives against hurting others, and, with the subjects' ears ringing with the screams of the victims, authority won more often than not. The extreme willingness of adults to go to almost any lengths on the command of an authority constitutes the chief finding of the study and the fact most urgently demanding explanation.'

Stanley Milgram (1974)

In all, just under two-thirds (65 per cent) of Milgram's volunteers continued to the highest level of shock, 450 volts, and all reached 300 volts. Milgram concluded that we have an overwhelming urge to obey an authority figure.

Milgram debriefed his volunteers, and explained the experiment to them. He found three types of subject:

- Some obeyed but sought to justify their actions. They shifted responsibility on to the experimenter or even the student (for being stupid).
- Some obeyed and blamed themselves. They felt bad about what they had done.
- A few rebelled, putting the student's well-being above the demands of the experiment.

Varying the experiment, Milgram found that obedience levels were higher when the experiment took place in a lab at the university, the experimenter wore a lab coat and stayed in the same room as the teacher. They were lower if the experiment was conducted in a run-down office in the city, the experimenter wore ordinary clothes and was in a different room. Subjects were also much more obedient if they didn't have to press the switch themselves but could delegate the task of administering the shock to an assistant.

A shock box used in Stanley Milgram's experiments.

Milgram suggested that we have two different states: autonomous and 'agentic'. In the autonomous state, we make our own choices and take responsibility for our actions, acting according to our own values and standards. In the agentic state, we carry out orders with no sense of personal responsibility. When faced with a figure of authority, he claimed, most people undergo an 'agentic shift' from the autonomous to the obedient state and this can explain any number of atrocities committed in the name of 'following orders'.

The validity of Milgram's results have been queried, and psychologist Gina Perry, author of *Behind the Shock Machine* (2013), found significant problems with both his method and his reporting. But it still seems that a fair proportion of people will take obedience far enough to inflict seemingly serious harm on another. It may not be that there is an inner-Nazi in all of us, but that there is an alarming tendency to do as we are told, even if we doubt the morality or wisdom of the order.

Laying low and saying nothing

The tendency to conform to expectations without even being given orders, or to blend in with the crowd, has been demonstrated by other experiments, too. In Zimbardo's Stanford Prison experiment, 'prisoners' applied for parole when they could just have left. Parents visiting played in role even though they had not agreed to be part of the study.

In 1951, the Polish social psychologist Solomon Asch (1907–96) investigated more benignly how far people will compromise themselves to conform. He placed a subject

'Ordinary people, simply doing their jobs, and without any particular hostility on their part, can become agents in a terrible destructive process. Moreover, even when the destructive effects of their work become patently clear, and they are asked to carry out actions incompatible with fundamental standards of morality, relatively few people have the resources needed to resist authority.'

Stanley Milgram (1974)

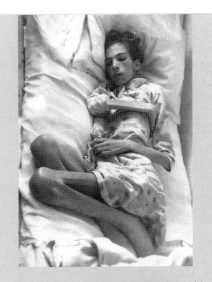

'Now that I look back, I realize that a life predicated on being obedient and taking orders is a very comfortable life indeed. Living in such a way reduces to a minimum one's own need to think.'

Nazi war criminal Adolf Eichmann (1960)

in a group with seven other people, and showed the group pairs of cards. In each pair, one card had a single line on it and the other had three lines of differing lengths, one of which matched the line on the first card. The participants had to say which of the three lines, labelled A, B and C, matched the single line. This was repeated many times. For the first set of trials, Asch's confederates gave the correct answer. Thereafter, they all agreed on the wrong answer – but they all gave their answers first, leaving the subject last to respond each time. Asch was interested to see whether volunteers would be swayed by the wrong answers given by others.

In a control experiment, a volunteer answered the questions alone and gave a wrong answer less than 1 per cent of the time, demonstrating that the task was easy.

However, when the confederates agreed on a wrong answer Asch found that 75 per cent of his subjects gave a wrong answer at least once. Interviewed later, participants who gave wrong answers fell into three groups:

- They actually believed the incorrect answer was true,
- They thought they must be wrong because everyone else agreed (Asch called this a 'distortion of judgment'),
- They realized everyone else was giving the wrong answer, but didn't want to look inferior or be the odd one out (Asch called this a 'distortion of action').

Of those who did not give the wrong answer, even though it set them apart, some acted confidently, some acted in a withdrawn way and some showed doubt but stuck with the right answer. When he varied the experiment, he found that if a single other person gave the correct answer, or if people could record their answers in writing rather than saying them aloud, rates of conformity with the wrong answer fell.

Smoke and accidents

Asch's experiment did not deal with a serious or threatening situation, but other experimenters have found high levels of conformity and reluctance to act independently even when that course of action produces danger. In New York in 1964, a woman called Kitty Genovese was attacked and murdered in front of 38 witnesses, none of whom (according to press reports at the time) came to her aid. The case sparked a significant psychological study into what was known as the 'bystander effect' – and which later came to be known also as 'Genovese syndrome', after the murder victim.

In 1968, American social psychologists

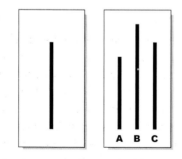

Subjects in Asch's experiment had to say which line on the right-hand card matched the line on the left-hand card.

John Darley (b.1938) and Bibb Latané (b.1937) set up an experiment to discover whether people would help a stranger in distress. They recruited volunteers who were told they were going to take part in a psychological study about personal problems

Murder victim Kitty Genovese.

and that because the issues discussed were private, the discussion would take place over intercom systems and the participants couldn't see each other. Part way through a discussion, one participant (an actor) faked a seizure, becoming increasingly distressed and saying they felt they would die. Other participants could hear this – and each other – over the intercom.

Darley and Latané found that the more people were involved in the discussion, the less likely it was that they would help. Even though they could not see the other participants, they knew they were there. It seemed that each person felt they had less responsibility towards the stranger in distress because there were other people around who should also feel responsible. In contrast, when a participant was the only person involved, they sought help 85 per cent of the time.

Darley and Latané carried out another experiment, this time apparently putting the participants in danger. They set students to complete questionnaires in a room. After a while, smoke started to leak into the room. The smoke got thicker and thicker until the students could hardly see. If students were alone when the room filled with smoke, 75 per cent reported the problem. But if they were in a room with two other people who ignored the smoke only 10 per cent raised the alarm. We assume that other people know more than we do and so if they are not responding to a crisis, we don't need to either. Psychologists call it 'pluralistic ignorance'. We would rather risk death than embarrass ourselves by raising a false alarm.

Join the group

There is an overt desire for conformity and to be part of a group. This was studied in 1967, not by a psychologist but an American history teacher, Ron Jones (b.1941), in Palo Alto, California. Jones had difficulty convincing his high school students that fascism took root so quickly in Nazi Germany so he started a movement, which he called 'The Third Wave', with the aim of overthrowing democracy. He made a convincing case for a different system being better able to deliver a high standard of performance and so greater rewards for individuals. The problem with democracy, he said, is that because it focuses on the individual, it reduces the strength of the group.

Jones had intended to run the experiment for one day only, but it was so successful that he continued with it. He added more authoritarian trappings, including a salute, and formal greetings that excluded non-members. Within three days, 200 students had joined and their academic performance

had improved. Some members started to denounce other members who broke any of the rules. On the fourth day, he felt it had got out of hand and would have to stop. He called the group to an assembly on the pretext that the national movement was about to be launched. Once they were gathered he told them it had all been an experiment and he showed them a film about the Third Reich.

As with Turner's theory of self-categorization, Jones' students were keen to define themselves in terms of the Third Wave group. They wanted to

assimilate the values they thought the group represented and have them as part of their personal identity. But Jones has demonstrated quite effectively that we all want to belong, and easily become, in Adolf Eichmann's words, 'one of the many

> '*Strength through discipline, strength through community, strength through action, strength through pride.*'
> Motto of Jones' Third Wave group

horses pulling the wagon', even if the wagon is on the way to hell.

Driven from within

The humanistic psychologists were more concerned with the empowerment of the individual than with group identity or what we all have in common. Yet on the path to self-actualization, we all have to meet other needs first, according to Abraham Maslow.

The pyramid of needs

In 1954, Maslow published a diagram that explained his theory of human motivation. The 'pyramid of needs' shows the hierarchy of needs that must be met, in order, on the path to 'self-actualization'. These needs, he maintained, provide the motivation for all human endeavour. Although Maslow produced his pyramid as a kind of road map for personal development, it demonstrates the universal human condition. What makes us a member of the human race is the drive to satisfy these needs, and what marks us out as individuals is the self-actualization we achieve at the end of the process.

At the bottom of the pyramid are the

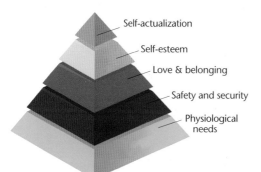

Self-actualization

Self-esteem

Love & belonging

Safety and security

Physiological needs

most fundamental physical needs – the need for food, water, sleep, air and basic bodily functions. Once these are met, we try to meet the need for security – both physical safety and the security that comes from having a stable job, a house, and so on. Next, we can move on to the need for love and belonging, met by having family, friends and sexual intimacy. This is followed by the need for esteem and respect, including self-esteem and confidence. With that need met, we can move on to self-actualization (see page 160–161).

Maslow differed from Plato and other philosophers and psychologists in that he recognized the baser needs and recommended meeting them, whereas many of his predecessors had said the needs should be suppressed, denied, or ignored in pursuit of higher ideals. For Maslow, the needs drive all human action and part of the

human condition – a good, productive part, for they spur us on to achievement.

Inside and outside the group

We all want to be individuals and yet we all want to belong, to be part of the group and not excluded. Self-actualization, if it comes, might make us feel comfortable to be different. But there are dangers involved in being different. One of those dangers is being considered mad. Those who have tried to be different, or have not tried hard enough to be like everyone else, have often been marginalized, demonized, pathologized and institutionalized. The flipside of trying to determine what the human mind is like is the discovery that some people are different.

The Greek philosopher Diogenes shunned property, living almost naked in an abandoned jar in the marketplace and eating scraps given to him by others. But he was self-actualized as this was how he wanted to live. Alexander the Great is said to have remarked that if he could not be Alexander, he would like to be Diogenes.

CHAPTER 8

Out of the
ORDINARY:
approaches to abnormal psychology

'I have of late, but wherefore I know not, lost all my mirth, forgone all custom of exercises; and indeed, it goes so heavily with my disposition that this goodly frame, the earth, seems to me a most sterile promontory...why it appeareth nothing to me but a foul and pestilent congregation of vapors...Man delights me not; nor woman neither.'

William Shakespeare, *Hamlet* (Act 1, Scene 3)

The Hungarian-born psychiatrist Thomas Szasz (1920–2012) suggested that people often have difficulties in life because they are not trying to live to the same pattern as the rest of us. They are the ones who have been classified as mad, disturbed, or mentally ill.

Madness is in the eye of the beholder – the 'mad' are not like us, and that's what makes us regard them as mad. There are now several ways of defining abnormal psychology that take account of criteria such as whether the person can function adequately in society, whether they are in distress, and how far they stray from 'normal' levels of mental health.

Facing page: The Scream *by Edvard Munch (1893).*

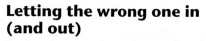

What's wrong with you?

As with physical illness, people can suffer acute episodes of mental illness or have a long-term, chronic psychiatric condition. Some people are born with minds that are different from the norm, just as some are born with bodies that are different, or mental problems can develop over time. This has been explained in three different ways: the supernatural (demons or spirits did it), the biological (there is a physical cause), and the psychological (mental events or conditions lie behind it).

> 'If you talk to God, you are praying; If God talks to you, you have schizophrenia. If the dead talk to you, you are a spiritualist; If you talk to the dead, you are a schizophrenic.'
>
> Thomas Szasz (1973)

Today, if you believe you turn into an animal once a month, you will be offered psychiatric help. In a different time and place, you might have been revered as a shaman.

Letting the wrong one in (and out)

In the absence of any better idea, mental illness has often been blamed on gods, spirits or demons. Even some of the otherwise enlightened ancient Greeks and Romans blamed madness on the action of the gods. After the fall of the Roman Empire around AD400, all physiological and psychological approaches to madness were forgotten and people reverted to superstition. By the early Middle Ages, the intellectual centre shifted to the Arabic and Persian world, where classical writings were translated and augmented. Middle Eastern doctors generally followed the Greek physician Galen in attributing mental distress to an imbalance of the humours (see page 186–187). For example, Ibn Sina considered that bestial madness, characterized by confusion, agitation, ferocity and behaving like a predatory animal, was caused by burnt yellow or black bile reaching the brain.

But non-academic Arabs continued to believe that madness was mainly due to supernatural factors, such as jinn (evil spirits or 'genies'). Indeed the Arab word for madness, junun, means possession by jinn. It could also be caused by the evil eye, by failing to observe rituals and taboos, by God, by non-supernatural means such as trauma, or by heredity.

In Europe, encouraged by the Christian church, with its panoply of demons and evil spirits, supernatural

The term 'mental illness' was first used in print in 1847 by Emily Brontë in Wuthering Heights, *and 'mental health' came into use in the early 1900s.*

BAD MAD WORDS

We no longer say people are mad. Some people now prefer the term 'mental distress', avoiding the stigma of illness. The past had no such sensibilities. Visitors paid one penny to see 'lunatics' – they did not pay to see 'mentally distressed people'. In the early part of the 20th century, the terms 'idiot', 'imbecile' and 'moron' had precise medical meanings. An idiot was someone with an IQ of 0–20; an imbecile had an IQ of 21–50; and a moron had an IQ of 51–70.

EPILEPSY – THE SACRED DISEASE

Epilepsy is now considered a neurological disorder, but for millennia its symptoms – seizures, loss of consciousness, drooling – were considered a sign of madness.

The earliest account of epilepsy is from Mesopotamia, written 4,000 years ago. The patient was said to be under the influence of a moon god and was exorcized. In the Babylonian Code of Hammurabi, written around 1790BC, if a person bought a slave who was then discovered to have epilepsy they could return him and get a refund. The condition was considered to be the result of evil spirits possessing the patient and was treated by supernatural means. The ancient Greeks associated epilepsy with good spirits and genius – they called it the 'sacred disease'. Hippocrates was a dissenting voice, saying that it was a physical disease in which heredity plays a part, but for once his views did not prevail. An association between epilepsy and spirits persisted into the 17th century in Europe. In Tanzania today, epilepsy is still considered to be caused by witchcraft or possession by evil spirits.

explanations of madness prevailed until the Enlightenment. Treatment of mentally ill people was often inhumane, the abuse intended to drive out the evil spirits assaulting or possessing them. The mentally ill were sometimes tortured and executed during the witch-hunts that claimed many lives in Europe and America between the 15th and 18th centuries. Displaying strange but harmless behaviours, such as mumbling,

A 1555 illustration of witches being executed. In Europe witchcraft remained punishable by law into the 18th century.

raving and repetitive actions, could be enough to bring a charge of witchcraft and death by hanging or burning.

But where there are bad spirits there can also be good spirits. Just as the Greeks considered epilepsy sacred, so some forms of apparent madness were considered to be divine inspiration or the presence of the Holy Ghost. In the 16th century, the Moorish author and historian Joannes Leo Africanus (1494–1554) wrote that in North Africa, 'There are certain people...whom a man would take to be distraughte, which goe bare-headed and bare-footed, carrying stones about with them, and these are reverenced by the common people, for men of singular holiness.'

A 9th-century illustration of an exorcism.

MOONSTRUCK

The word 'lunacy' originates with the Roman belief that some madness was caused by the influence of the moon or the action of the moon goddess, Luna.

MARGERY KEMPE (c.1373–1440)

The English mystic Margery Kempe wrote the first memoir or autobiography in English. She seems to have suffered some form of mental illness after the birth of her first child, perhaps post-natal depression or mania, as she records that she believed she was surrounded by demons. She also resorted to self-harm. Later, after experiencing a religious vision, she would frequently roar and rage in church, believing this to be the influence of the Holy Ghost. The Church appears to have agreed with her, as she was allowed to go on pilgrimages and sometimes encouraged to go to church and experience her 'visitations' without being accused of witchcraft or unnatural behaviour.

A HISTORY OF HYSTERIA

Hysteria is now known as histrionic personality disorder (HPD). It is characterized by excessive displays of emotion, attention-seeking, inappropriate sexual displays or behaviour, self-dramatizing and theatrical behaviour, being easily impressed, manipulative, egocentric, often emotionally shallow and changeable. It affects 2–3 per cent of the general population in the USA. More women than men are diagnosed with it.

The ancient Egyptians were the first to mention hysteria. In the Ebers papyrus, dating from 1900BC, it is linked with the uterus. The ancient Greeks continued this belief; Hippocrates, who was the first to use the term hysteria, said that it was caused by wayward movement of the uterus (*hysteron*) due to too little sexual activity. It was not until the 17th century that the uterus was let off the hook. The English physician Thomas Willis (1621–75) suggested that the brain and nervous system were at the root of hysteria, and that meant that men could also suffer from it.

The German physician Franz Mesmer (1734–1815) treated patients with hysteria using his technique of mesmerism, a form of suggestion. In the 19th century Jean-Martin Charcot used hypnosis with his hysteric patients. Charcot influenced Freud, who accounted for hysteria by saying that it occurs when the individual's libido does not evolve as it should

do. There has been some suggestion recently that HPD is not a psychological disorder at all but a kind of cultural disorder. By this account, people diagnosed with HPD are being so labelled because they don't conform to the prevailing behavioural norms rather than because they have a mental condition.

Biology and the brain

Hippocrates dismissed supernatural accounts of illness. He taught that there are physical causes, most commonly an imbalance of the four humours, that could affect mood and behaviour as well as having physical effects. He made an exception for hysteria (see panel).

A mind unbalanced

The Greek physician Asclepiades of Bithynia (c.127–40BC) dismissed humoral theory as the cause of psychological distress, laying the blame on emotional problems. So did the Swiss physician and alchemist Paracelsus (1493–1541), who thought a chemical imbalance was responsible, as he was able to treat his patients using herbal preparations. He saw the body as a chemical system that must be kept in balance with itself (the 'microcosm'), and with the larger environment (the 'macrocosm').

Paracelsus divided mental problems into five classes:

- epilepsy
- mania
- chorea lasciva (lascivious behaviour)
- suffocatio intellectus (suffocation of the intellect)
- true insanity (those permanently insane with no periods of lucidity or remission).

He said that epilepsy is caused by the *spiritus vitae* (spirit of life) boiling and rising to the brain. He recommended a herbal remedy in cases that were not entrenched, but said sometimes epilepsy is present from birth (a

view he shared with Hippocrates). Mania he ascribed to some kind of humour that rises up the body and collects in the head, where part of it condenses and part remains as a vapour.

Neither *chorea lasciva* nor *suffocatio intellectus* is clearly described. He mentions three types of *suffocatio intellectus*: one is caused by intestinal worms, one afflicts only women and is caused by malfunction of the womb (presumably hysteria), and another is a sleep disorder. He also cites several causes of *chorea lasciva* including recklessness and disgraceful living (exemplified by being a whore or enjoying guitar music):

'Thus, the cause of the disease chorea lasciva is a mere opinion and idea, assumed by imagination, affecting those who believe in such a thing. This opinion and idea are the origin of the disease both in children and adults. In children the case is also imagination, based not on thinking but on perceiving, because they have heard or seen something. The reason is this: their sight and hearing are so strong that unconsciously they have fantasies about what they have seen or heard.'

Paracelsus (published posthumously in 1567).

Paracelsus gave a taxonomy of mental illness that also included five 'true insanities'. These were melancholy (depression); lunacy caused by the moon; permanent insanity caused by eating or drinking (something poisonous, presumably); those who were born insane, either because they inherited insanity from a parent or because the 'seed' was defective; and, finally, those who are possessed by demons. This is the only mention he makes of demonic possession and he doesn't elaborate upon it.

Working with humours

Paracelsus was something of a maverick. Most people who sought a physical source of mental distress followed humoral theory, even in the 19th century. Humoral theory gave a way of categorizing mental disorders by aetiology, or cause. So depression (melancholy), resulted from an excess of black bile. Consequently, treatments were aimed at reducing the preponderance of black bile, usually by purging and bleeding the patient.

The methods of diagnosing humoral imbalance included listening to the patient's own account of their troubles and daily life, and examining and even tasting the blood and urine to determine the type of humoral imbalance.

Paracelsus.

THE ANATOMY OF MELANCHOLY

The first full-length textbook on depression, *The Anatomy of Melancholy*, was published in 1621 by the English scholar Richard Burton (1577–1640). It is an encyclopaedic tome that ran to 900 pages in its first edition, and Burton continued to extend it throughout his life. The style is arcane and rambling; it is stuffed with classical quotations and references and covers myriad topics only slightly related to depression. Even so, Burton distinguished between routine misery caused by life events ('reactive depression', as it would be called now) and entrenched melancholy ('clinical depression', in modern terms). He described 'Melancholy in disposition' rather long-windedly as:

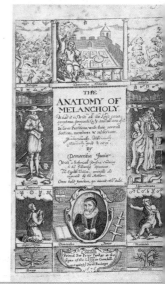

'...transitory Melancholy which goes and comes upon every small occasion of sorrow, need, sickness, trouble, fear, grief, passion, or perturbation of the mind, any manner of care, discontent, or thought, which causes anguish, dulness, heaviness and vexation of spirit, any ways opposite to pleasure, mirth, joy, delight, causing forwardness in us, or a dislike...'

The other type of melancholy (clinical depression) is 'melancholy of habit' and is the main subject of his book:

'This Melancholy of which we are to treat, is a habit, a serious ailment, a settled humour, as Aurelianus and others call it, not errant, but fixed: and as it was long increasing, so...it will hardly be removed.'

> 'The melancholike man...is afraid of
> everything...he would runne away
> and cannot goe...he is become
> as a savadge creature haunting
> the shadowed places, suspicious,
> solitarie, enemie to the sunne, and
> one whom nothing can please, but
> only discontentment, which forgeth
> unto itselfe a thousand false and vain
> imaginations.'
>
> Anatomist Andreas Laurentius
> (1558–1609)

The brain revealed

Eventually a link began to emerge between the physical state of the brain and some forms of mental disturbance. The most striking case study was that of railroad worker Phineas Gage.

Gage suffered a terrible accident in 1848 when working as a construction foreman on the railroads in Vermont, USA. A tamping iron – a long, pointed metal rod – was fired accidentally through his head, entering his skull through the cheek, leaving through the top of his head, and destroying much of the left frontal lobe of his brain on the way. The stalwart Gage apparently sat upright in an ox-cart for the journey to town, and chatted helpfully to his doctor. Gage was not expected to live and yet made a miraculous recovery. But he is said to have suffered a personality change, becoming offensive and rude. Although there are conflicting reports, these changes seem to have been temporary.

Contemporary psychologists seized on Gage as an example, although his case did not show much that was conclusive except, perhaps, that removal of the frontal lobe need not be fatal. He was used as an illustration by phrenologists in support of their theories that the Organ of Veneration and/or the Organ of Benevolence was destroyed and this accounted for his subsequent rude behaviour (but not for the fact that it corrected itself over time). He was also used to demonstrate that there is no localization of function in the brain, as he was later capable of doing pretty much everything he could do before – even with most of the left frontal lobe missing. Clearly, these two conclusions are mutually exclusive.

The theory of localization of brain function gained apparent support in 1861. The French surgeon Paul Pierre Broca (1824–80) discovered an area of the

Phineas Gage holding the tamping iron that injured him. Gage lived for another 12 years after his accident – part of which he spent working as a stagecoach driver in Chile.

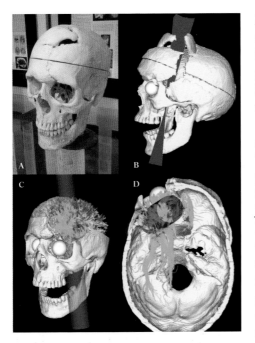

Gage's skull (A) and a computer modelling of the path of the tamping iron through Gage's head (B, C and D).

brain, now known as Broca's area, that is responsible for speech. Broca's discovery came about when he carried out a post-mortem on a patient, Leborgne, who had lost the ability to speak and could say only one word, 'tan'. Broca found a lesion in the frontal lobe of the brain caused by syphilis. A second patient, Lelong, could say only five words; Broca found the same area of the frontal lobe was damaged.

Since then, more areas of the brain responsible for particular functions have been discovered. Modern imaging methods such as PET scans and MRI scans have been used to show which areas are at work when particular tasks are performed and to compare the sizes of structures in different brains (see page 85 [Chapter 3:

Route masters]). The abnormal size or level of activity of part of the brain is sometimes implicated in particular types of abnormal psychology. Further, DNA sequencing has turned up links between some gene variations and abnormal psychology.

All in the mind

The first thorough approach to psychological causes came with the work of Sigmund Freud and the Austrian physician Joseph Breuer (1842–1925). According to Freud, all disturbances in the adult mind are the result of past trauma, usually originating in childhood, that has been forgotten or repressed. His theory was that previous physical and mental or emotional experiences produce our mental states and that after deep conversation with a therapist who 'analyses' the patient, the problem can be brought to the surface and defused (see page 202 [This chapter: *It's all talk*]).

The importance of sex

Freud decided that all neurosis stems from an incident in childhood that involves sexual abuse ('seduction', usually by an adult). Early in his career, he claimed that he had uncovered such sexual episodes in all his patients. Much later, he changed his tune and said that the sexual abuse did not necessarily happen, but was present as a memory or a fantasy in each patient and that had the same effect. In fact, none of his patients had recalled any instance of childhood sexual abuse prior to their treatment.

Freud regarded every aspect of human behaviour as being driven by libido, which he considered specifically a sexual drive.

THE KILLER WITHIN?

The American neuroscientist James Fallon (b.1947) made a particularly striking discovery in 2006. While studying brain scans of psychopaths and, separately, Alzheimer's patients, he discovered that his own brain matched the profile he had developed of psychopathic brains. (He had used his own brain scan as a control in the Alzheimer's study.) It had lower than normal levels of activity in areas of the frontal and temporal lobes associated with empathy. When he looked at genetic indicators, he found he also had a variant of the MAO-A gene linked with psychopathy. Investigating his family history, Fallon found that he was related to several convicted murderers, and the notorious Lizzie Borden, accused (but acquitted) of murdering her parents with an axe in 1892. He concluded that he is a pro-social psychopath: ambitious, high-achieving, but not dangerous. A different upbringing, though, might have turned him into a full-blown serial killer.

Lizzie Borden.

Many of his most influential and erudite followers parted company with him because he placed sex at the centre of all his work. Most felt, not unreasonably, that there could be other drives and incidents that affected behaviour and mental health. Carl Jung and Alfred Adler were the most famous of the defectors. One psychologist who stuck by him throughout was his daughter, Anna Freud.

Dissenting voices

The German–American psychologist Hugo Münsterberg (1863–1916) studied many people with mental illness in his attempts to understand the causes of abnormal behaviour. He had no patience with Freud's psychoanalytic approach, though, and made no attempt to investigate a patient's past or unconscious motivation. Instead, he encouraged patients to expect an improvement in their condition and believed that improvement would then follow. He considered genuine psychosis to be untreatable, though, as he thought it was caused by degenerative damage to the nervous system and so was a physiological, rather than psychological, problem.

The behaviourist John B. Watson also saw mental illness as the result of early experiences, but not through undergoing a process of internalization and festering, as Freud would have it. Watson argued that many of the so-called symptoms of so-called mental illness were conditioned reflexes in which the conditioning was counterproductive. He was interested in particular psychoanalytic tools, such as word association tests, which he thought could allow one to trace the origins and precise nature of the twisted habits that manifested as mental illness.

Moving on

Although some of Freud's work has been discredited, the idea that early experiences leave a lasting impression and affect later psychological states is now rarely disputed. Freud's one-time colleague Adler developed his own theory, that feelings of inferiority or superiority arose in childhood (see page 145 [Chapter 6: *Building 'you'*]). Today, a massive psychotherapy industry is based around the general premise that how one is treated as a child and later life experiences can have a lasting and sometimes damaging effect on the psyche.

FREUD'S PROBLEMS WITH SEX

Psychosexual stages: Freud believed that all children go through stages in their early development when they gain sexual pleasure from different areas of the body, called erogenous zones. During the first year, the oral stage, the erogenous zone is the mouth. The baby gains pleasure from suckling and exploring objects with his or her mouth. During the next year, the erogenous zone is the anus as the baby learns bowel control. From the ages of two to five, the genitals are the erogenous zone. Freud called this the phallic stage, which he applied to boys and girls as he considered the clitoris a type of mini-penis. Arrested development in any of these stages could, he believed, lead to particular types of personality or disorder. Freud focused on three aspects of the developing mind as especially significant:

Oedipus complex: Children of both genders, Freud claimed, develop an intense sexual attraction towards their mothers during the phallic stage. In boys, this Oedipus complex grows into competition with the father for the mother's affection and the fantasy (latent, at least) of killing the father and replacing him. The name is taken from the Greek legend of Oedipus.

Castration anxiety: The boy sees his father as more powerful than himself and as the source of his feelings towards his mother is his penis, he develops castration anxiety – he is afraid his powerlessness will be physically manifested.

Penis envy: The girl notices her father possesses something valuable – a penis – which she does not have. She envies him this, but as she can't have it, she 'becomes' her mother and shares him instead.

Counting the ways

In the 2nd century BC, Asclepiades of Bithynia distinguished between acute and chronic psychological disorders and between hallucinations and delusions. An acute episode could occur after bereavement or other loss; the depression would pass as they adjusted to their loss. A chronic condition could be permanent insanity or unremitting mood disorder.

The Roman author Aulus Cornelius Celsus (c.25BC–c.AD50) provided the earliest use of the term insanity (or 'insania') in his *De medicina*, written around AD30. He distinguished between the different types by the patient's behaviour:

'There are several sorts of insanity; for some among insane persons are sad, others hilarious; some are more readily controlled and rave in words only, others are rebellious and act with violence; and of these latter,

*An illustration from a 1657 edition of Celsus'
treatise* De medicina *(On medicine).*

some only do harm by impulse, others are artful too, and show the most complete appearance of sanity while seizing occasion for mischief, but they are detected by the result of their acts.'

He gave accounts of people who thought they were gods, famous figures, inanimate objects, or animals; of epilepsy and of paranoia; and distinguished between the hallucinations caused by fever and genuine delusions.

The Roman medical philosopher Aretaeus (AD50–130) recognized the pattern of bipolar disorder: periods of depression alternating with periods of mania or excitability, with periods of lucidity in between. He campaigned for humane treatment of the mentally ill, realizing that it was not only those of limited intelligence who can have mental health problems.

In the 10th century, the Arabian physician Najab ud-din Muhammad identified thirty different types of mental illness, including agitated depression, neurosis, sexual impotence, psychosis, schizophrenia, mania, priapism, obsessive-

In Shakespeare's Macbeth, *Lady Macbeth's
hallucinations represent her loss of sanity.*

compulsive disorders, delusional disorders and degenerative diseases.

The Swiss physician Felix Platter (1536–1614) outlined several different types of mental disorder including mania, delirium, hallucinations, foolishness and obsessive unwelcome thoughts (which would now be considered an aspect of OCD, Obsessive Compulsive Disorder).

As with physical illness, the same symptoms can have many different causes. It is no more sensible to assume that everyone suffering hallucinations has the same mental condition as that everyone sneezing has the same physical illness.

Before Kraepelin, doctors had listed the symptoms of several hundred forms of mental illness, but he took a different

> '[In cases of melancholy,] imagination and judgment are so perverted that without any cause the victims become very sad and fearful. For they cannot adduce any certain cause of grief or fear except a trivial one or a false opinion which they have conceived as a result of disturbed apprehension…This frightful melancholy, which often drives men to despair, is the most common form of melancholy. In curing it I have been frequently very much impeded. They have often confessed to me with many tears and deep sighs, with the greatest anguish of heart and with their whole body trembling that, when seized by this, they have felt themselves driven toward blaspheming God and committing many horrible things, toward laying violent hands on themselves, killing their husbands or wives or children or neighbours or rulers, not out of motives of jealousy and not out of envy toward them, whom rather they fondly love, but out of an involuntary compulsion. They say that such thoughts creep up on them against their will and that they continually and urgently call upon God to deign to free them from such impious thoughts.'
>
> Felix Platter (1602)

From symptoms to syndromes

The first thorough attempt at classification came in the 19th century. The German psychiatrist Emil Kraepelin (1856–1926) studied psychology with Wundt. He wanted to categorize mental disorders as thoroughly as Wundt had categorized sensations, and to that end he spent years studying patients with mental disorders, determining the course, outcome and prognosis of different conditions.

approach, which he called clinical. Instead of grouping together cases that shared major symptoms, Kraepelin used patterns of symptoms, or syndromes, as the basis of his classification system.

One of his most important contributions was to divide mental illness into two categories. The first he called 'manic–depressive psychosis' (now called bipolar disorder), which recurs at regular intervals. The second he called 'dementia praecox' (premature dementia), because it usually appeared in early adulthood, it never went away and was degenerative. It was first described by the French physician Philippe Pinel (1745–1826) in the late 18th century. It was renamed schizophrenia in 1908 by the Swiss psychiatrist Paul Eugen Bleuler (1857–1939) when he determined that the dementia was a secondary symptom and decline did not always occur.

Kraepelin pioneered psychopharmacology – studying the effect of drugs on the nervous system – researching the impact of substances including morphine,  coffee and alcohol. He expected that there would be a physical or genetic marker for all conditions, though these were not then known. An unfortunate consequence of his conviction that many mental disorders had genetic origins was that he was a supporter of eugenics, feeling the world would be a better place if these 'problems' were allowed to die out through restricted breeding.

The categorization of mental disorders undertaken by Kraepelin inspired the *Diagnostic and Statistical Manual* (DSM), which is used now by many psychiatrists to diagnose patients with mental problems. With increasing understanding of the structure, chemistry and biological processes of the brain, some mental health problems can now be explained more precisely – but not necessarily cured.

Care, cure and containment

Mental disturbance can range from neurosis that disrupts a person's daily life to full-blown psychosis that makes them incapable of normal life. Clearly these require different types of treatment, though the treatment of mental distress always has been – and remains – difficult and often unsuccessful. In an ideal world, doctors could offer a cure. But more often, care or – at worst – containment has been the only provision for those with mental health problems. Many people in mental distress have been left untreated and either cared for by their families or left to wander from place to place, vulnerable and dependent on the goodwill of others. No doubt many came to a premature sticky end.

NEUROSIS AND PSYCHOSIS

Psychosis involves losing touch with reality. Some mental illnesses are marked by periods of psychosis between long or short periods of lucidity. A few people are permanently out of touch with reality. Neurosis is an exaggerated response or concern with some aspect of living that causes anxiety, distress or obsession.

Dealing with demons

The best way to counter something with supernatural causes was often thought to be by supernatural means, such as incantations, talismans and prayers. Sometimes, the supernatural methods would appear to work as the person got better (whether by coincidence or suggestion), so reinforcing belief in the supernatural cause and cure. But treatment was not always as benign as using an incantation or talisman – it could be brutally physical, even in its supernatural aims.

The oldest known treatment is trephination. The 'surgeon' would bore a hole, or cut out a portion of the skull, using a knife or drill made of animal bone, shell, rock or metal. Trephination could have been used to treat headaches or fits, or to release spirits. The earliest surviving trephined skulls are Neolithic – about 10,000 years old. Around two-thirds show evidence of bone regrowth, showing that the patient survived for a considerable time. Some have been trephined repeatedly. Trephination is not limited to the distant past. The French physician Arnaldus de Villanova (1235–1313) advocated trephination to let both demons and bad humours escape from the brain, and the practice is still used in some parts of Africa, South America and Melanesia.

An ancient Greek suffering from mental or physical health problems in the 4th century BC might choose to visit a temple dedicated to the medical god Asclepius. He or she would first offer prayers and sacrifices and then sleep in a dormitory (a practice known as 'incubation'), hoping to be visited by dreams that would guide the priest/physician towards suitable treatment. Non-venomous snakes slithered freely around the floor of the dormitory, and were used in healing rituals – hence the snake in the snake-and-staff emblem, the Rod of

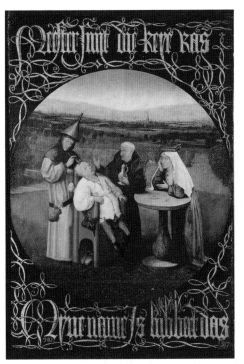

The Extraction of the Stone of Madness *by Hieronymous Bosch (c.1494).*

Asclepius (the Greek God of healing), that has come to be associated with medicine. The physician's job was to interpret the patient's dreams correctly. Treatment might include medication with herbs, special diet, baths, massage or other physical treatments.

In the medieval Arab world, treatment was often enlightened (see page 197), but could also include exorcism and cautery (burning) applied to parts of the body. In 13th century Anatolia, exorcisms were performed by dervishes. In Europe, too, exorcisms might have been attempted to save a person infested with demons – if they were not simply categorized as a witch and quickly despatched.

It would be nice to think that superstitious treatments have ended entirely, but they are still going strong in some places. The only psychiatrist in Chad, Dr Egip Bolsane, still has to tell his patients to stop believing in witchcraft.

Getting physical

Physical treatments for mental illness rely on there being some kind of connection between ghost and machine. The predominant model throughout European history has been some attempt to rebalance the humours.

Humouring the humours

With the ancient Greeks, humoral theory led to some gentle and some invasive physical therapies. Many of the treatments Hippocrates recommended could have been beneficial: a healthy diet, lots of sleep, a regime of exercise and activity, pleasant baths and other gentle types of therapy. Others were less pleasant and probably less beneficial. Over the next two millennia, much harm was done through excessive blood-letting and purging.

Asclepiades of Bithynia, in the 2nd century BC, argued for sympathetic treatment of the mentally ill. He disapproved of bleeding, and of locking away people who were disturbed. Instead, he promoted natural treatments such as massage, diet and music therapy, with different styles of music recommended for patients with different mental states. He also advocated a swinging hammock to soothe distressed patients to sleep. The early Arab hospitals provided a combination of pleasant and unpleasant treatments for the mentally ill

according to what was suitable for the patient's condition. This could be emetics, bleeding with cups or leeches, and baths. These treatments countered the excess of bile in the brain, either by removing it from the body (bleeding and emetics) or by diluting it (supplying extra moisture).

Paracelsus didn't follow the humoral model, but for all that some of his treatments were distinctly unpleasant. For mania, he suggested two treatments, one of which is

'If, however, it is the mind that deceives the madman, he is best treated by certain tortures. When he says or does anything wrong, he is to be coerced by starvation, fetters and flogging. He is to be forced both to fix his attention and to learn something and to memorize it; for thus it will be brought about that little by little he will be forced by fear to consider what he is doing. To be terrified suddenly and to be thoroughly frightened is beneficial in this illness.'

Celsus, 2nd century AD

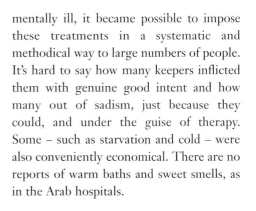

barbaric, involving skinning of the fingers and toes (or other parts) either chemically or surgically so that the 'vapours' can escape. The alternative consists of taking medicines, and we can imagine would have been more popular with patients. *Chorea lasciva*, which he considered characterized by lascivious behaviour, he treated first by shutting the patient in a dark room with little food or water. If that didn't work, a sound beating was called for, and finally – for the most intransigent cases – he recommended throwing the patient into cold water.

Many of the brutal treatments inflicted on patients in madhouses and asylums from the 17th to 19th centuries were intended to help rebalance the humours, including blood-letting, purging (using emetics), starvation diets, and enforced cold baths. With the rise of institutions to house the mentally ill, it became possible to impose these treatments in a systematic and methodical way to large numbers of people. It's hard to say how many keepers inflicted them with genuine good intent and how many out of sadism, just because they could, and under the guise of therapy. Some – such as starvation and cold – were also conveniently economical. There are no reports of warm baths and sweet smells, as in the Arab hospitals.

Hospitals for the mentally ill

One of the greatest achievements of medieval Islam was the founding of hospitals. No one was turned away on account of their inability to pay, and hospitals were open to both men and women. The earliest firm evidence of a hospital making provision for the mentally ill is from Cairo, Egypt, in AD872 by Ahmad ibn Tulun, the Abbasid governor of Egypt. Many more followed, it becoming standard practice for Islamic hospitals to provide for the mentally ill. In 1183, the traveller Ibn Jubayr described the Nasiri hospital in Cairo:

'*A third [building]…is a large place, having rooms with iron windows; it serves as a place of confinement for the insane. They also have persons who daily examine their condition and give them what is fitting for them.*'

There were tranquilizing medicines, such as opium, and calming music and massage. The

The 'Scene in Bedlam' from William Hogarth's A Rake's Progress *(1732–33).*

intention was clearly care and cure, though he did later report that a hospital in Damascus had 'a system of treatment for confined lunatics, and they are bound in

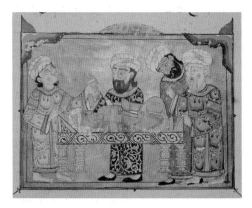

A doctor visiting his patient, from a 14th-century Persian manuscript.

chains', apparently to protect the medical staff and patients. Some talking therapy, too, seems to have been current. The Persian physician Abu Bakr Mohammad Ibn Zakariya al-Razi (AD865–925), known in the West as 'Rhazes', advised doctors to help patients drive trifling matters about which they obsessed from their minds and build up their reasonable thoughts. Music, dramatic performances or readings, and prayer were also available to the patients.

Humane treatment in Islamic mental hospitals continued for many centuries. The Turkish travel writer Evliya Çelebi (1611–c.82) recorded his visit to a hospital next to the Bayezid Mosque in Edirne, Turkey. He described a type of olfactory therapy with flowers, and remarked that a troupe of singers and musicians visited three times a week to play to the patients.

Out of sight with the out-of-mind

While in Arab countries, mentally ill people could receive hospital treatment, in Europe those without family support wandered from place to place, begging for food.

Then, towards the end of the Middle Ages, a few small Christian institutions such as monasteries began to care for – or at least keep – the mentally ill along with paupers and the physically sick. People who could not care for a mentally ill relative could turn to the parish for help. The parish might provide a nurse, or board the mentally ill person in a special boarding house. Over time, these grew into private madhouses.

Bedlam

The Priory of Saint Mary of Bethlehem, founded in 1247, is now better known as

'Some rooms are heated in winter according to the nature of the sick...Those brought to the asylum by the police are fettered by gilded and silver chains around their necks. Each one roars and sleeps like a lion in his lair. Some fix their eyes on the pool and the fountain and repeat words like a begging dervish. And some doze in the rose garden, grape orchards and fruit orchards...and sing with the unmelodious voices of the mad.'

Evliya Çelebi

King Lear's mad raging through the countryside in all weathers was not atypical of the fate of the mentally ill.

Bedlam. Originally a hospital for paupers, it began to take in mentally ill patients and by 1403 had six patients classified as insane. There were four pairs of manacles, eleven chains, six locks and two pairs of stocks that could have been used to restrain patients. By 1460, it had made the transition to being purely a mental hospital.

For some centuries, Bedlam was run by 'keepers' with no particular medical knowledge or interest and who used the position for personal profit. The patients were kept in deplorable conditions, often starving and with few or no clothes. In 1598, an inspection by the governors found it 'so loathsomly filthely kept [it is] not fitt for anye man to come into the sayd howse.' There were at the time 21 inmates, none of whom had been there for less than a year; one had been an inmate for 25 years.

Booming business

During the 17th century, the number of private madhouses grew rapidly. Many, Bedlam included, opened to the public, and viewing the 'lunatics' became a tourist attraction. At a charge of a penny a time, it was an important source of revenue. Another source of revenue was taking in anyone, mad or not, that someone else wanted to be rid of.

The conditions for inmates were often appalling. Many were kept permanently shackled, chained to walls, often lying on straw in their own filth, starving and freezing, with few or no clothes or bed-coverings. Medical interventions included bleeding, beating and immersion in cold water. The gyrating chair, invented in the 18th century, was used to whirl the patient around at up to 100 revolutions a minute. It could be used in darkness for extra effect. The idea was to shake up the blood and tissues and restore equilibrium but it actually resulted in loss of consciousness and sometimes bleeding from the ears, nose and mouth.

In 1815, the case of a patient called James Norris brought conditions in Bedlam and other mental hospitals to public notice

The Maniac *by Thomas Rowlandson (1787).*

James Norris spent twelve years in solitary confinement in Bedlam, chained to a metal bar with his arms pinioned. No details of the 'act of lunacy' for which he was sent to Bedlam were recorded. Six members of parliament who visited him all found him sane, lucid and capable of conversation. His case sparked reform in Great Britain.

and an inquiry eventually led to the reform of madhouses.

A better way: from madhouse to asylum

Reform movements in the 18th and 19th centuries sought to put an end to the worst excesses in the madhouses. New methods, pioneered by the Italian physician Vincenzo Chiarugi (1759–1820), the English physician William Tuke (1732–1822) in England and Philippe Pinel in France, treated patients humanely. They were not chained or beaten, and did not have to work. If restraint were necessary, straitjackets or fabric bands reinforced with metal were used, rather

> 'It is a supreme moral duty and medical obligation to respect the insane individual as a person.'
> Vincenzo Chiarugi, *On Insanity* (1793–94)

than shackles. These were not madhouses but asylums, intended for care and, where possible, cure. The activist Dorothea Dix (1802–87) campaigned (successfully) for similar reforms in America in the mid-19th century.

Philippe Pinel, as physician at the Bicêtre Hospital in Paris in 1793, worked with the unofficial governor, a former patient called Jean-Baptiste Pussin, to 'enrich the medical theory of mental illness with all the insights that the empirical approach affords'. They replaced bleeding, purging, and blistering with close personal contact and careful observation. His patients were unchained and Pinel engaged in long conversations with them. The method was clearly psychiatric. Pinel constructed detailed case histories that helped him to categorize different types of mental illness.

The age of asylums

The work begun by Chiarugi, Tuke and Pinel wrought a sea-change in the way the mentally ill were cared for. The 19th century saw dramatic social changes in Europe and America. Cities grew rapidly, and lifestyles changed. Vast, stately asylums sprung up to care for the mentally ill who could no longer be cared for by their families. The new asylums were built on a grand scale:

'Conceive a spacious building…airy, and elevated, and elegant, surrounded by extensive and swelling grounds and gardens. The interior is fitted up with galleries, and workshops, and music-rooms…all is clean, quiet and attractive…'

The ideal was to restore people to health by gentle methods, but the reality fell far short. Mentally ill people were removed entirely from their families because it was thought the best chance of cure came with 'removing the lunatic from all his habitual pastimes, distancing [him] from his place of residence, separating him from his family… surrounding him with strangers, altering his whole way of life' (French psychiatrist Jean-Etienne Esquirol, 1772–1842). Rigorous 'treatments' continued, or resurfaced,

A social occasion at the Colney Hatch Asylum, Middlesex.

including bleeding, purging, and cold baths and showers.

The number of inmates increased by a factor of ten over the course of the 19th century and, by 1890, the asylums had sunk again into deplorable conditions. They were overcrowded and had returned to using straitjackets, seclusion and sedative drugs such as bromide to control disruptive or combative patients. Most people admitted to an asylum stayed there until they died. Again, reformers began to speak out against the asylums, and again conditions in the asylums fell until, in the second half of the 20th century, many were closed, putting responsibility for care back on the community.

Brave new treatments

The mental hospitals continued to fill up through the 19th and 20th centuries. In the first half of the 20th century, optimistic faith in science led to a clutch of radical treatments for mental illness. Patients were subjected to invasive and often experimental procedures including massive doses of insulin, electric shock treatment (later known as electroconvulsive therapy, ECT), prefrontal lobotomy, raising the body temperature to 41°C, or putting patients into a drug-induced sleep for days or weeks at a time.

ECT was introduced in 1938 by Italian neuropsychiatrists Ugo Cerletti (1877–1963) and Lucio Bini (1908–64). It consists of passing an electric current through the brain, causing convulsions. Relief of symptoms is considerable after 10–20 treatments, which are usually given twice or three times a week. Drugs to induce convulsions had been used previously, with the first reported use in the 16th century, when convulsions had been found to reduce symptoms in severely depressed and schizophrenic patients. ECT as it was first given could result in broken arms and legs as the patients thrashed around, but was later given with muscle relaxants and anaesthetic. ECT declined when better drug treatments for depression and schizophrenia emerged in the 1950s, accelerated by the negative public image of the treatment fostered by the 1962 novel and 1975 movie *One Flew Over the Cuckoo's Nest*. ECT is still used, as long as patients give informed consent,

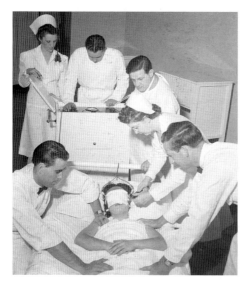

Electroshock therapy, c.1942.

and is considered a valuable treatment of last resort.

If ECT seems extreme, it's not as bad as a prefrontal lobotomy, another experimental method inflicted on many unsuspecting and probably unconsenting patients. It involves destroying much of the connection to the prefrontal lobe of the brain. The technique was first found to make chimpanzees docile; three months after this result had been reported, the Portuguese neurologist António Egas Moniz (1874–1955) began tests on human subjects. He, rather dubiously, won a Nobel Prize in 1949 for this controversial form of surgery.

It's all talk

Quite the opposite of the drastic physical treatments that emerged in the 20th century is the 'talking therapy' developed first by Sigmund Freud.

In his psychoanalytic method, diagnosis and treatment progress together. Talking at length with a psychoanalyst both uncovers the problem and, by enabling the patient to bring it out and examine it, reduces its negative impact and begins healing.

Freud's contribution

Freud developed the 'talking cure' into the full-blown psychoanalytic method, championed it, and is generally associated with it. His method has become part of the therapeutic repertoire, and still informs analysis techniques today.

From 1885–86, Freud studied in Paris with the great hypnotist Jean-Martin Charcot. Charcot believed that hysteria could be triggered, at least in part, by psychological causes. On his return from

NOW YOU SEE IT – BUT WHAT IS IT?

Callosotomy involves the cutting of the corpus callosum, which connects the two hemispheres of the brain, resulting in so-called 'split-brain' patients. It is sometimes used to treat intractable epilepsy. In experiments with split-brain patients, Roger Sperry discovered that an item seen with the left eye only cannot be named. This is because the information from the left eye goes to the right side of the brain, but the left side of the brain is, for most people, used for speech control. With no connection between the two halves of the brain, the left side can't know what the right side has seen and so can't name it.

Paris, Freud began in private practice in Vienna, specializing in hysteria and using hypnosis. But he ran into problems. Some patients could not be hypnotized. Others refused to believe the 'recovered memories' they had revealed under hypnosis, so he could make no headway. He eventually tried another method. He had patients lie on a couch, close their eyes and recount their experiences of a symptom. He found that simply talking was usually enough to get them past any resistance. He had developed the method known as free association – and, by chance, the enduring icon of psychoanalysis: the analyst's couch.

Freud likened psychoanalysis to an archaeological dig. From just a few remaining fragments, the archaeologist pieces together the landscape of an ancient city; from a few recalled fragments, the analyst pieces together the patient's psychological landscape.

THE CASE OF ANNA O.

The method of psychoanalysis originated with the treatment of 'Anna O.' (actually Bertha Pappenheim). Twenty-one years old, Anna had suffered a range of physical symptoms including partial paralysis, eating disorders, speech disturbances, disorientation and memory loss while and after caring for her father during his long, final illness. She was diagnosed with 'hysteria' and treated by Joseph Breuer (1842–1925), initially using hypnosis.

Each time Breuer got her to recall when she had first experienced a symptom, the symptom disappeared, at least temporarily. Breuer concluded that some ideas or memories were too painful to bear conscious scrutiny and so were manifested in physical symptoms instead. When the suppressed energy of the distress was dissipated through talking about it, the correlating symptom was no longer needed and vanished.

Breuer saw Anna O. for around 1,000 hours over 18 months. Although he considered her cured, she was to spend a considerable time in a mental institution and took large amounts of morphine for her continuing pain. Years later, as a successful social worker, she strongly resisted any suggestion that those in her care be psychoanalysed.

Later researchers have often concluded that Anna O.'s problems were in fact neurological and so were never going to be cured by psychoanalysis. It was Anna O. who first coined the term 'talking cure'.

MIND'S END

The story of psychology is still very much under way – we are not far from the opening pages and have no idea how the story will end.

The mind-body problem, first fully articulated by Descartes, still lies at the heart of psychology, not only unresolved, but further complicated by the work of the intervening years. We could now speak of a mind-brain-body problem, or even a thinking-mind-brain-body problem. Just as the contents of a book are not the same as the physical object of the book, so the mind and its contents and functions are beginning to be prised apart. Cognitive scientists focusing on the algorithmic or computing model of the brain, and neurologists looking at its mechanics and chemistry, have helped to separate mental activity from the mind itself.

Our conception of the 'mind', after Freud, has to take account of unconscious as well as conscious mental activity. As we begin to look at the brain with electronic equipment, we find stunning results – such as the apparent making of a 'decision' before we are consciously aware of it. This throws into doubt the role of the conscious mind and the existence of freewill.

Into the future

Today, psychiatry depends on a combination of drug treatments, talking therapies and, occasionally, some form of psychosurgery. By no means all patients can be helped. And it's still not really clear how we should define abnormal psychology and whether we can distinguish it.

ON BEING SANE IN INSANE PLACES

In 1973, the American psychologist David Rosenhan (1929–2012) carried out an experiment with rather terrifying results. He sent eight healthy people (including himself) to psychiatric hospitals in the USA where they faked auditory hallucinations. All were admitted as patients. After admission, they acted normally and said they had no more hallucinations. The average time they spent in hospital was 19 days, and all had to admit to having a mental disorder and agree to taking antipsychotic drugs before they were allowed to leave. All but one was diagnosed with 'schizophrenia in remission'. After an outcry from the psychiatric profession, Rosenhan accepted a challenge from one hospital to send imposters over a period of a year and they guaranteed they would recognize them. Over the course of the following year, of 193 new patients, 41 were identified as potential Rosenhan fakes. In fact, Rosenhan hadn't sent any patients at all. He concluded, 'It is clear that we cannot distinguish the sane from the insane in psychiatric hospitals.'

The one and the many

Each of the schools of psychological thought attempts to look in a particular way at why we are as we are and act as we do. But the schools are largely incompatible. Psychology has fragmented into myriad different approaches and studies, sometimes in conflict and sometimes simply coexisting.

A few psychologists, including Gregg Henriques of Vermont University, seek a 'unifying theory' for psychology that will bring it together. The standard model of the atom, general relativity and quantum mechanics provide a framework within which physics currently operates. Biology has evolution and genetics which, together, can account for the ways organisms work and develop. Psychology is without a frame of reference on which all practitioners agree and within which developments and ideas can be assessed and tested. Some psychologists say that such a unifying theory is not possible. The fundamental split between the behaviourist and mentalist schools means there is not even agreement on whether the mind exists, let alone how we might study and measure it in valid ways.

It's likely that as time passes, more and more will be discovered that links mental states and acts with neuroscience and brain chemistry. That might offer new ways of understanding and treating abnormal

psychology. But it's unlikely that it will fully explain the mental – what it feels like to be in love, hear music, or engage in a creative act. We might never be able to say why any particular individual will prefer one political theory to another, believe in God or dislike sport. Noam Chomsky believes that some problems are beyond the capability of the human brain to comprehend. The nature of our own minds might fall into that category.

> **IS FREEWILL AN ILLUSION?**
>
> Itzhak Fried, working in California and Tel Aviv, reported in 2011 that by monitoring an electrode implanted in the brain he could 'see' subjects making a decision to press a button a second and a half before the subject believed they decided. From the electrode information, Fried could predict with 80% accuracy which choice the subject would make. Apparently, the 'decision' is made somehow in the unconscious mind and represented in the conscious mind as an act of freewill after it has already been determined.

> 'My hunch … is that the answer to the riddle of free will lies in the domain of potential science that the human mind can never master because of the limitations of its genetic structure… In principle, there are almost certainly true scientific theories that our genetically determined brain structures will prevent us from ever understanding.'
>
> Noam Chomsky, 1983

Index